EVERY

BODY

COUNTS

Barbie Latza Nadeau

EVERY
BODY
COUNTS

MONEY, LIES, AND
THE HIDDEN TRADE
IN HUMAN LIVES

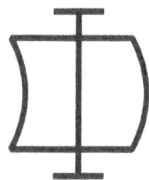

ITHAKA

First published in the UK in 2025 by Ithaka Press
An imprint of Bonnier Books UK
5th Floor, HYLO, 103–105 Bunhill Row,
London, EC1Y 8LZ

Owned by Bonnier Books
Sveavägen 56, Stockholm, Sweden

Hardback – 9781804186473
Trade Paperback – 9781804188125
Ebook – 9781804186480

A CIP catalogue of this book is available from the British Library.

Typeset by IDSUK (Data Connection) Ltd
Printed and bound by Clays Ltd, Elcograf S.p.A.

1 3 5 7 9 10 8 6 4 2

MIX
Paper | Supporting
responsible forestry
FSC® C018072

Every reasonable effort has been made to trace copyright holders of material
reproduced in this book, but if any have been inadvertently overlooked
the publishers would be glad to hear from them.

www.bonnierbooks.co.uk

Dedicated to all the many victims of human trafficking whose stories will never be told

CONTENTS

INTRODUCTION

An attractive young woman in her mid-20s sits on a dove-grey armless sofa in the London headquarters of a famous international bank. She's impeccably dressed in a robin's-egg blue dress and heels. She could be a high-flying graduate trainee, investing money from her first job. Or maybe she's taking out a mortgage to buy her first property, with a deposit financed by her well-heeled parents. Or perhaps she is just here to open an account.

The bank clerk calls her name and holds open the frosted glass door for her. She shows her ID document, signs a piece of paper, and pushes it back towards the banker. He hands her a receipt, which she folds without looking at it and neatly tucks into her designer handbag. They speak politely for a few minutes, and then she stands up. They shake hands. She walks out of the bank to a waiting car. Perhaps it's her driver, or a boyfriend?

Inside the car, the illusion ends. Her handler takes the piece of paper from her. She is driven to a luxury apartment with doors that are kept locked from the outside, and returns to a daily routine of forced prostitution for wealthy clients. She never enjoys the earnings that are deposited into the bank account opened in her name. To make her account seem legitimate, her traffickers make transfers labelled 'rent' and 'bills'. All the while, she is effectively a prisoner, and even though her name is on the account, she cannot independently withdraw the money because she is not allowed to do anything on her own.

As she sits in the bank's office, it seems like it should be easy for her to ask for help, to tell the bank clerk what's really happening, tell someone in the lift about what she is made to do every day. But it is too risky. She could be thrown into prison, or deported. And, as she has been warned a thousand times, no one will believe her anyway.

If the bank account manager had paid closer attention, he might have realised something was off. Where does all the money flowing into her account every month originate from? Why does it come from so many different payees? And why is she transferring so much of it to someone else?

But he doesn't ask. No one raises the alarm. She's just another victim hidden in plain sight.

* * *

Walk down any street in any major city in the world and human trafficking is omnipresent. Look closely at the person giving you a manicure at the nail bar. Consider who picked the vegetables you see in the supermarket. Look around the waiting room at the medical centre offering private organ transplants. Open your closet, your cupboard, your phone. Who is taking care of your children, or cleaning your house? You don't have to be a trafficker to participate in the trafficking economy.

Trafficking in persons, or human trafficking, is a form of modern slavery – the terms are used to describe the forced movement, or restriction of movement, of people to do things they don't want to do for the profit of the trafficker. Some countries, like the

UK, consider modern slavery and human trafficking as separate albeit intertwined crimes, with trafficking in humans a subset of modern slavery (see, for example, UK Research and Innovation's website). The United States' Department of State and the European Union (for example, in the European Parliament's report on forms of slavery) use the terms interchangeably (as this book does) in relation to criminal investigations, as do groups working to identify, rescue and rehabilitate victims. By conservative estimates, modern slavery affects between 40 and 50 million people, according to a 2022 United Nations report, only slightly less than the entire population of England.

Human trafficking is a complex crime which, along with the intertwined evil of forced labour, nets around $150bn a year for its perpetrators, according to an International Labour Organization report from 2014 – a sum slightly more than the annual global investment in fighting the effects of climate change. But unlike the climate crisis, which is widely acknowledged to require urgent international action, there is a negligible amount of government money invested in stopping trafficking. Often, efforts to combat it come from the private sector, like airlines in the United States, or from nonprofit groups like Stop the Traffik in the UK.

There have been attempts to address trafficking internationally. In 2000, the United Nations Office on Drugs and Crime (UNODC) adopted the first legally binding protocol – often referred to as the Palermo Protocol, after the Italian city where it was first signed – as part of the United Nations Convention against Transnational Organized Crime. By 2023, 181 countries had signed the protocol, promising they would provide protection and assistance to victims of human trafficking and ensure that their rights are fully respected. Before that, countries approached the issue in a more ad hoc way, with policies varying widely between nations.

The 2000 protocol was supposed to change all of that. It didn't. 'Despite tremendous expenditure, a majority of anti-trafficking efforts initiated after the Palermo Protocol have broadly failed to achieve their core mission and sustain longer-term, positive impact, as evidenced by the ever-increasing number of victims worldwide,' Michael Gallo, a public policy researcher who collected data during the first 20 years of the protocol wrote in a damning analysis on its 20th anniversary. 'Trafficking is not an isolated incident, nor can we easily disentangle how, where and why it occurs without consideration of matters such as labour rights, climate change, internal displacement, transnational migration, discrimination and human agency' (United Nations University Institute, Macau, 2020).

It's not easy to define what kind of person is susceptible to being trafficked because so many factors overlap depending on the country from which they are being trafficked and the country into which they are trafficked. In the last UN Global Report in Trafficking in Persons, published in 2022, 51 per cent of the victims were in financial need; 25 per cent were children, often growing up in dysfunctional family situations. In the US, 72 per cent of trafficking victims were also identified as migrants. In Europe, where the demographics of victims are measured differently among the 27 member states, International Organization for Migration (IOM) surveys reveal, according to *The Guardian* (18 October 2016), that 70 per cent of all migrants arriving in Europe by boat from North Africa are trafficked. European border countries like Italy tend to focus first on migration status rather than whether arrivals are victims, while other countries that do not see an influx of irregular migration, such as Norway, have stronger programmes in place to help victims.

And it is on the rise. Human trafficking is the fastest-growing criminal industry in the world, second only to drug trafficking, as revealed in a fact sheet published by the Washington, DC Attorney General's office. Organised crime syndicates are increasingly turning to human trafficking to make their profits, in part because the supply of desperate people on the move is also growing. And these criminals can find ways to make money from migrants that go beyond straightforward trafficking. 'Migrants are more profitable than drugs,' Salvatore Buzzi, a mob boss in Rome, was caught saying on wiretap prior to his 2017 arrest for skimming off public funds that were supposed to be for providing accommodation for asylum-seekers. Modern slavery has grown by 10 million people since 2021, according to the International Organization for Migration (IOM). Tragically, child trafficking remains very much part of the picture: 30 per cent of all detected trafficking victims are children, and the majority of these are trafficked for sexual exploitation, according to ChildX.

The success of trafficking relies entirely on the availability of vulnerable people to traffic, starting with the more than 280 million people who are on the move around the world at any given moment. While many of these migrate using officially recognised paths and are motivated by 'pull' factors like opportunities for education or work, many others are pushed from their homes by wars, famine, economic strife and, increasingly, climate change, according to the IOM. As the global number of would-be migrants grows, developed nations tighten their border controls and offer fewer legal opportunities to immigrate, driving aspiring migrants towards irregular routes. Hopeful, but often desperate, the individuals on these treacherous journeys are some of the most vulnerable people on earth. Because when human beings leave all they know behind, they become targets for exploitation.

* * *

'People trafficking' is a modern term, barely used before the 1990s. But the forced movement of humans across borders, and their sale and purchase, is a crime as old as time. Slavery, abduction and the trade in humans has marked many family histories, in ways both obvious and hidden.

I discovered this for myself when a cousin investigated our family tree. My grandfather's family emigrated to the US from nineteenth-century Bohemia. But my cousin's search for his mother's origins unexpectedly led to the border between Afghanistan and what was in the 1800s British India. We discovered that our great-grandmother, as an infant, had been removed from Afghanistan by Catholic missionaries and sent to the Austrian empire.

The more I learned about human trafficking, which can occur under the umbrella of adoption, the more I wondered about the circumstances in which my great-grandmother was spirited away from her family in a village in Afghanistan in the mid-1800s. Was she really 'saved' by a Jesuit missionary in the Catholic Church, or was she 'given' to a wealthy Catholic family, perhaps one prepared to make substantial contributions to the Church? Her birth certificate was created at the time of her adoption. There is no record of her biological mother's death. Her personal history was always vague, the details never quite clear, and it seemed to change based on the teller. She had simply been told the Catholic family who raised her mother couldn't have children of their own; and the rest is history, incomplete as it is.

When I moved to Italy in 1996 and began working as a journalist for *Newsweek* magazine, I found myself reporting on irregular immigration into Italy, which was a subject I, like many foreigners in the country, had scarcely been aware of. Silvio Berlusconi had just been elected prime minister, and his relationship with Libya's authoritarian leader Muammar Gaddafi was woven into almost all the geopolitical stories I was chasing at the time. I particularly remember when Gaddafi would come to Rome and pitch his Bedouin tents in the city's luscious gardens. And I can't forget how he threatened to 'open the spigot to turn Europe black' – a racist statement with a not-so-veiled threat. The spigot he referred to was his grasp on Libya's ports, which in the mid-1990s were just starting to fill up with sub-Saharan Africans hoping to cross the sea to a better life.

I spent time in migrant camps and shelters, and was on one of the first non-governmental organisation (NGO) rescue boats that started patrolling the waters in the mid-2000s. It was then I noted the number of young Nigerian women among the other migrants, which marked an increase in sex trafficked women on the streets, first in Italy, and eventually across Europe and the United Kingdom. My book *Roadmap to Hell*, published in 2016, dissected the close relationship between the Neapolitan Camorra and Nigerian mafia groups that control the trafficking.

I met many young Nigerian women who told me they had been sold into slavery by their families. Knowing this cast a particular light on my family history. There is a substantial likelihood that, if she wasn't stolen, my great-grandmother was sold by an impoverished family. It's a devastating thought, conjuring up images of Dickensian villainy. Yet, as I knew from my reporting work, thousands of babies and children are still sold today, as revealed in a *Deutsche Welle* report in 2024. The lucky ones are raised by infertile couples who love them. But others are forced to be sweatshop workers, or sex workers, like the young women I met.

When my great-grandmother was taken from her mother, she left her history – our history – behind. That missing history is what first drove me to try to understand the plight of migrants and refugees who wash up on the shores of Italy, the country I emigrated to willingly, and to dig into the murky world of people smugglers and traffickers. This book tells the stories of those who live in this world, where lives don't matter, but where every body counts.

* * *

Despite efforts to fight the scourge, today there is nowhere in the world where trafficking is adequately prosecuted, according to UNODC. If it were, there would be better deterrents for the criminals all along the chain. Instead, lack of meaningful investigation is an enabling force that keeps the cycle of criminality alive.

Laws against trafficking do exist, but they are rarely enforced. In 2022, the EU logged more than 8,000 suspected traffickers, but fewer than 2,000 were convicted. Charts show that the number of victims and suspects consistently rises, but the number of convictions has never topped 2,000, according to a 2024 Eurostat report. In 2009, UNOCD said:

> The response to human trafficking in terms of number of convictions recorded per year is still weak, especially compared to the number of victims that are estimated to be trafficked in Europe, which is estimated to be around

250,000 per year. Most European countries record national conviction rates for human trafficking below one convict per 100,000 people.

The fact that smugglers and traffickers work largely unhindered across the world has fed a deadly industry. Tragedies are common, from Europe's coastline to the English Channel to the Darién Gap. In 2022, authorities stopped an 18-wheel refrigerated articulated lorry on a routine stop near the US border with Mexico. When they opened the trailer, they found 47 dead bodies and 19 survivors, 12 of whom were children—human cargo worth at least half a million dollars. Four people later died in hospital, making it the single worst migrant smuggling disaster in US history.

Alongside the lack of prosecution, another great boon for traffickers is the distrust and xenophobia that is often directed at their victims. No country offers automatic immigration rights to people who have been trafficked illegally across borders, despite the Palermo Protocol, which was meant to guarantee such protection. Instead, authorities in the most popular destination countries are frequently so preoccupied with trying to stem the flow of irregular immigrants that they do not look for victims.

In a best-case scenario, victims should be able to apply for protection under a victims of trafficking protocol, but in many cases, identifying themselves to authorities would risk immediate deportation, or even incarceration. Beyond this, victims of trafficking frequently do not have the means to escape in the first place, unless they are identified by law enforcement or an anti-trafficking group.

Ultimately, groups like Human Rights Watch, the United Nation's refugee agency, and the IOM say that the best way to attack the business of trafficking would be to offer clearer and more accessible opportunities for people to apply for asylum in their home countries, to avoid them falling into traffickers' traps in the first place.

* * *

Irregular migration, which is – frequently erroneously – also referred to as 'illegal migration' is an incendiary topic, and the subject of endless political posturing. Irregular migrants are commonly depicted as sexual deviants and thieves, or used by the media and politicians as bogeymen to seed fear among voters that migrants will take their jobs and taxes. In the United States, Donald Trump famously promised to build a wall to prevent migrants, whom he characterised as 'drug dealers, criminals and rapists' (BBC, 31 August 2016), entering the country. In Italy, Giorgia Meloni won the 2022 elections by promising to 'stop the boats', implying that she would do it at any cost. In her more radical days, she even advocated sinking the boats (InfoMigrants, 27 October 2020). In the UK, as reported by *The Guardian*, in June 2024 Nigel Farage tried to smear Keir Starmer by saying he 'fought very, very hard for those that arrive on the back of lorries to get benefits once they got here'.

While only a fraction of irregular migrants cross the English Channel compared to those who enter Europe across the Mediterranean Sea or those who enter the US from Mexico, there has been rapid growth in Channel crossings since 2018. Media coverage tends to focus on the overall number of irregular migrants landing in the UK without examining the underlying structures that enable their arrival. Awareness of the roles played by people smugglers and traffickers is growing – Prime Minister Keir Starmer talked of 'smashing the gangs' in his 2024 election campaign. But so far there has been little public in-depth analysis of how organised crime and exploitation impact the numbers of irregular migrants arriving on British shores.

The global trade in human lives is intercontinental. According to the *New York Times*, South American drug cartels make around $13bn a year smuggling migrants into America, many of whom are trafficked. During research for my 2022 book *The Godmother*, I was astonished to discover that the Italian Mafia makes twice as much as the South American cartels working with North African gangs to move hundreds of thousands of people across the Mediterranean Sea each year. And across Asia, young women and men are trafficked for sex on a staggering scale. In Thailand alone, there are thought to be about 610,000 modern-day slaves – about one in 172 of its population of 69 million – according to the Global Slavery Index.

The trafficking industry has a symbiotic relationship with the black market. Russia, India and China are known for having sizeable black markets specialising in manufacturing, buying, selling and trafficking high-tech weapons, gold, medicines, drugs and human bodies – but, expressed as a percentage of GDP, the UK, the US and European countries, including Greece, Italy, Spain, and even Norway and Germany, also have sizeable shadow economies, according to a 2017 *Forbes* report. These markets remain out of sight a lot of the time, and measuring them is complex and not an exact science. Financial investigators use techniques including random checks and comparing reported income to reported spending to find discrepancies. Products sold on the black market often end up being traced only when the damage they cause becomes public, such as when people overdose on opioids bought without a prescription. Similarly, human trafficking victims are frequently only discovered on the back of another incident, for example if a sweatshop burns down or a sex worker is killed.

Undocumented workers make up the most exploited segment of the workforce in many sectors, because they often don't qualify for legal protection after entering a country illegally or over-staying their visas. For the one hiring them, it's an opportunity to sideline taxes and pocket more money. For the worker, there are no protections and no guarantees. They are disposable, and those who hire them know it. Migrants grease the wheels of the underworld.

But it's not the underworld alone that benefits from trafficked people. As this book will show, trafficking is only possible through the widespread complicity of the financial sector, the tourism sector, the fashion industry, agricultural enterprise, the medical community, governments who look away and, in some cases, even well-intentioned NGOs.

Trafficking is a truly international phenomenon. While some victims are trafficked within their home countries – a significant problem with complex causes and impacts – this book will focus on those who are trafficked across borders, in particular along some of the most popular irregular migration routes in the world. The UK and US are particularly popular as final destinations. Countries that lie along regional frontiers, like Italy, Greece, Spain, Mexico, Libya, Tunisia, and locations like the Calais camps in France, are transit regions where the businesses of both smuggling and trafficking thrive. Other countries become transit regions intermittently as geopolitical situations escalate, as when Turkey received an exodus of Syrian refugees in 2011, many of whom crossed to Greece and were eventually given asylum in Europe.

Sometimes, as in the case of Tunisia in recent years and Libya during the Arab Spring uprisings, local violence fuelled by government instability drives emigration from these countries. But the citizens of transit countries are rarely the majority of those people trying to leave. For example, Libyans made up less than 1 per cent of those who try to enter Europe by sea in the last five years, according to Italian government statistics. In 2024, the most common nationality of people crossing the English Channel route from Europe and Asia to the United Kingdom was Vietnamese, according to government statistics, many of whom will be trafficked for the forced marijuana cultivation racket in the country. The most common nationalities of people crossing the Mediterranean from North Africa in 2024 were Bangladeshi and Syrian; and people from Venezuela, Ecuador and Haiti made up the largest demographic of people crossing the Darién Gap route into Mexico and the United States, according to the US Council on Foreign Relations.

Of course, not all migrants who cross borders illegally are victims of trafficking. Many migrants freely trying to enter a country illicitly employ the same smugglers that traffickers use. The difference between people trafficking and people smuggling is consent, according to the IOM, which makes clear distinctions between the two criminal entities. 'Migrant smuggling involves consent – those being smuggled are receiving a service they requested in exchange for payment,' the IOM states.

However, once someone enters the irregular migration economy, they become intensely vulnerable to abuse. A situation that seemed to be under the traveller's control descends into one of coercion, creating a blurred line between the two categories. As the IOM goes on to point out: 'Many smuggled migrants – notwithstanding that they began the journey voluntarily – become victims.' Typically, traffickers will arrange for a migrant to be moved between countries, but that movement is later used against the trafficked person, who is told they 'owe' the trafficker compensation for their travel, and is kept in bondage.

If the smuggled or trafficked person reaches the destination country and is apprehended by the authorities, there is frequently little distinction made between those who made the journey freely and those who did not. In fact, trafficking victims may end up being arrested for the crime of human trafficking or manslaughter themselves, such as those who are coerced into captaining smuggler ships across the English Channel or Mediterranean Sea and incarcerated on arrival for trafficking.

Widespread ignorance about the underlying power structures of people smuggling and trafficking allow criminal enterprises to drive deadly migration attempts with impunity. Consider this fact: someone becomes a new human trafficking victim every thirty seconds, as revealed in a 2013 US President's Advisory Council report, yet fewer than 1 per cent of traffickers are successfully prosecuted, according to UNODC.

On a practical level, the difference between trafficking and smuggling is that smugglers make money from the movement of people from point A to point B. Traffickers work in a bigger sphere, recruiting the person from their home country and supplying them to meet demand, usually, but not always, in a richer economy. Traffickers employ smugglers to move their victims for them, usually paying them upfront. While the smuggler gets a one-off fee, the trafficker gains a resource that they can exploit for profit again and again.

This explains why smuggling is decisively not where the big money is. It accounts for only a fraction of the trafficking and forced labour industry's $150bn yearly profit. Governments trying to stop 'trafficking' by focusing on smugglers will never succeed, any more than stopping drug runners has worked to harm cartels, or stopping small-time thieves has worked to stop organised crime syndicates.

As well as smugglers, traffickers also rely on brokers to find victims. Brokers are go-betweens, acting as liaisons when a trafficker needs a certain commodity: prostitutes, vegetable pickers, organs, embroidery seamstresses, domestic workers. Trafficking is not a static enterprise. It is seasonal and constantly changing, based on factors like geopolitics, border clampdowns and climate change. For example, droughts in southern Europe curtailed labour trafficking for agriculture in 2023 because there were simply fewer crops to harvest.

The broker is the most visible link in the hierarchy and will often go out and help find the people to fill smugglers' boats in person. They generally operate in transit cities and port towns where smugglers work, and can easily identify people who fit the ever-changing needs of traffickers. It is often a broker who commissions the smugglers to move migrants across borders, in order to deliver them to their clients, the traffickers. They also have extensive Facebook and Telegram channels aimed at desperate migrants thinking about making a move, and utilise the Dark Web.

It's not surprising that it is a lot easier for authorities to identify and apprehend smugglers and brokers than traffickers. They are more exposed, often less experienced, and much more likely to be the first in line when things go wrong. In 2015, authorities in Austria found an abandoned truck emblazoned with pictures of chickens and sausages on the side of a rural highway near Parndorf. It caught their eye because of the blood streaming from under the locked doors. At first, authorities naturally thought the overwhelming stench of decomposition was from the carcasses of rotting chickens, but after prying the doors open, they discovered the bodies of 71 dead migrants from Syria, Iraq and Afghanistan who were being smuggled overland into Europe on the Balkan route, which is the primary land smuggling route into Europe. Among them was a baby under a year old.

Police immediately launched a Europe-wide manhunt for the driver who had abandoned the truck. A surveillance video identified the man driving the truck as Mitko, a Bulgarian broker who lived in Hungary. An Interpol investigation revealed that Mitko had secured the transport of the 71 people for around $3,000–$5,000 a person, depending on where they were from. His human cargo was to be delivered to a trafficker in Munich, who would determine which of them could be trafficked onward to the UK for forced labour in various sectors. But when his primary driver—the smuggler—failed to show up for the job to take the migrants to Munich, Mitko had no choice but to drive them himself, or risk losing the payment from the trafficker.

What Mitko, who was normally just a broker, didn't realise was that the back doors of the truck had to be kept slightly ajar to allow air into the airtight refrigerated unit. Mitko instead locked the doors tightly, immediately cutting off all ventilation.

As is often the case in land smuggling endeavours – especially the particularly lucrative ones – a follow-up car accompanied the truck to help the driver escape if they ran into trouble. According to surveillance footage collected during the investigation, at a certain point, Mitko heard screams and banging from inside the vehicle, which prompted him to stop alongside the road. But he didn't open the back doors for fear the victims inside might try to escape. His backup car driver agreed they should abandon the vehicle.

The chicken truck was found at least two days after it had been abandoned. When authorities finally sealed and then towed the vehicle to a refrigerated warehouse for forensic investigation, they determined that most of the people had died within an hour of the doors being closed. They also noted that the truck had standing room only. Those inside were packed so tightly, the dead would have taken their last breaths wedged among the living. The screams and banging must have come from those on the perimeter.

Despite their deadly mistake, the traffickers running the scheme were no amateurs. 'This was not the first nor the last human trafficking organised by this group,' Zoltan Boross, head of Hungarian police's anti-trafficking unit, said during a press conference. 'That vehicle required a very serious logistical background, with very serious money and a very serious circle of people.' Investigators discovered that the transportation of the victims was paid for in advance and the total of around $328,000 went to Mitko's boss, a 30-year-old Afghan man living in Bulgaria. This leader of the trafficking ring escaped prosecution, but later died in an earthquake in Morocco in 2023. He had been helped by another broker, Sediq Sevo, who eventually went into hiding in Iraq, from where he boasted to Reuters by phone, 'I have good experience in the smuggling industry ... I have been working for more than seven years in the smuggling sector ... I used to take people from Kurdistan to Turkey and from Turkey to Greece all on foot and by car.'

In contrast to sea migration, where smugglers rarely get on the boats themselves, land smugglers are often directly involved in the transport of people, in theory making them easier to prosecute. But they can also provide cover for more powerful associates; land smugglers, when caught, tend to take the fall for the entire ring, including for the traffickers, who with rare exception never physically participate in the movement of their victims. In some cases, migrants may be hidden in containers and cargo crates unknown to the driver, or at least that's what many drivers of trucks have often insisted. This cuts out the middleman, but it does not cut out the trafficker frequently still waiting for them to arrive.

There is one more part that completes the puzzle of victims, traffickers, smugglers, brokers and other associated middlemen that makes up the trade in humans: the consumers, as detailed in a 2014 article in the *Revue internationale de droit pénal*. From those who knowingly purchase sex from victims, to employers who turn a blind eye to forced labourers, to shoppers who unwittingly buy products made with slave labour, the trafficking economy couldn't exist without them. Or, I should write: without us. This book examines how we can face up to the reality of trafficking, and help to end it.

CHAPTER 1

SEX AND MONEY

A brief history of trafficking

The victims of trafficking are not always recognisable, even to those who work trying to aid them. They will rarely identify themselves to potential rescuers, not least because traffickers warn their victims to be wary of people pretending to help but who will abuse them even more severely. A Nigerian sex-trafficked woman I met in Italy once told me that her captor showed her newspaper clippings about priests and even nuns raping children to dissuade her from trusting religious figures who might offer aid. When nuns approached her she was initially terrified, though she later accepted their help. It is easy to understand the dilemma. As badly as a victim might be treated, his or her traffickers are sure to use tactics that make them unlikely to trust other strangers.

Trafficking victims come from many countries and backgrounds, but frequently follow the same trajectory:

- First, they are vulnerable, sinking under the weight of poverty, fleeing violence, or unable to find work.
- Next, they are hopeful, often believing the trafficker is really a saviour who is offering them an opportunity.
- Ultimately they are trapped, having lost their freedom to exploiters who effectively own them.

It would be a mistake to think that all trafficking victims are desperate or easily fooled – sophisticated traffickers are able to recruit victims from all walks of life. One of the most impressive women I have ever met is Blessing Okoedion, a Nigerian sex trafficking survivor who I met at a shelter in Caserta, Italy, where she was helping a nun called Sister Rita get girls who had suffered a similar fate to her off the street.

Blessing was a college-educated computer science programmer who answered an advertisement for a job in a computer shop in Spain. The supposed company arranged to fly her to Madrid and get her through Spanish border control. But once she got there, her so-called employers took her documents and told her she was being relocated to Italy. Against her will, she was taken to Castel Volturno on the Via Domitiana in Campania. She was beaten, raped and forced to work on the street. Defying her captors, she demanded clients take her to the police. Finally, one of them did so and she was eventually rescued, testified against her traffickers, and started her own NGO.

Back in Nigeria, Blessing had been aware that women from her country were often forced into prostitution in Europe. Even so, she fell prey to such a scheme by simply believing someone had legitimately hired her. Today, she often speaks at events, does outreach in Nigeria, and travels to other countries from which young women – and, increasingly, young men – are trafficked.

Dehumanising people who are trafficked is one of the most important tools the trafficker has. If a victim is made to feel that she or he deserves maltreatment, it's easier to keep them subdued, and harder for them to find or accept help. I've met women who felt so demeaned they didn't believe they even deserved to be saved from sex trafficking rings. They were raped relentlessly and beaten physically, but still had to try and find the energy to attract customers. If not, they would be punished at the end of the night, often with psychological abuse and further gang rape.

Of course, there are women – and men – who freely choose to engage in sex work, who have regular health checks, who maintain normal lives when they aren't working and who keep all their earnings. But sex trafficking victims are those who are deprived of their liberty, who live outside the law, whose health and safety are constantly at risk, and who see almost none of the money they make.

No matter how destitute the victim, each person forced into prostitution is worth tens of thousands of dollars to the trafficker who 'owns' them. And trafficking can be highly bankable. In the summer of 2023, US prosecutors investigating money laundering uncovered a lucrative sex trafficking ring that ran from Boston to northern Virginia. Two Korean-American citizens, Han Lee, 41, and Junmyung Lee, 30, and American Jamie Lee, 68 – not related – were arrested for running an exclusive brothel that catered to politicians, tech executives, pharmaceutical executives, lawyers, professors and military officers, according to the Justice Department.

The scheme was complex and the profits were impressive. Around 250 women, mostly Asian, were trafficked for sex at apartments in Cambridge and Watertown in Massachusetts, and in Fairfax and Tysons in Virginia. Han Lee has been charged with being the mastermind behind the business. Born in South Korea and naturalised in California, she is accused of trafficking women to the US on false promises through her connections in Asia. Investigators found a pair of Louis Vuitton shoes worth $1,360 in the apartment in Cambridge, along with luxury bags from Yves St Laurent,

Givenchy, Christian Louboutin and Jimmy Choo, along with money order receipts worth more than $1m, and an 'impeccable' ledger in which she kept the brothel business accounts.

Junmyung Lee had purchased a 2018 Corvette with his profits, and investigators also found receipts for expensive clothing and travel in his apartment. James Lee was arrested in California, and charged with leasing all the apartments used as brothels under his real and assumed names. He allegedly flew from California to Massachusetts and Virginia to sign the leases and took a cut of the profits made in them. 'In exchange for opening the leases in his identity, or his fraudulent ones, James received $1,000 per month for each brothel location that remained open,' the affidavit reads. 'A review of bank records for his co-conspirator, Han, revealed that he in fact received at least $64,000 from her, which is believed to be compensation for placing the brothel leases in his name, or in his fake identity.' The eldest of the three is also charged with fraudulent activities related to COVID government assistance, which he allegedly applied for under the names of his fake businesses.

The three who were arrested are accused of renting expensive apartments in mainstream complexes for upwards of $3,600 a month. Appointments were made via text message, with confirmations sent and directions given remotely. The pimps offered what amounted to a 'menu' of options for what they wanted to do with the women, including a minimum one-hour guarantee. The clients had to pay cash upfront to enter the room.

The individuals who were charged deposited all the profits in their personal bank accounts, often buying money orders so as not to draw attention to large cash deposits. Rent in the apartments was also paid by money order, to avoid tying any of the culprits to the apartments used for the illegal sex trade. The trials are ongoing at the time of writing.

The women sold in the brothels were advertised with nude photos on the websites bostontopten10.com and browneyesgirlsva.blog. Buyers could choose the women, who were described by height, weight and bust measurements, and then book an appointment for sex at a luxury apartment at rates starting at $600 an hour. The photos were professionally taken and the websites also offered nude Asian models for photo shoots for advertising and marketing purposes, which the Justice Department deemed a cover-up. New women frequently appeared in the advertisements.

Some of the sex workers in the ring are believed to have been trafficking victims, but regardless were charged with irregular immigration and prostitution crimes. At the time of writing, none of their 'wealthy and well-connected' clientele had faced charges.

* * *

Stories of sexual exploitation like those of Blessing or the high-end brothel network's victims are shocking, but they still represent only the tip of an iceberg.

The term 'human trafficking' is often mistakenly thought to refer primarily to sex trafficking, and while it is true that sex trafficking delivers the lion's share of the industry's profits, it by no means involves the largest number of people. The International Labour Organization (ILO) estimates that $99bn of the annual return of $150bn is made on sex-related exploitation. But just 22 per cent of the world's trafficking victims are forced into prostitution or other forms of sexual exploitation. The ILO estimates that 68 per cent of trafficking victims worldwide are exploited for labour and the rest fall into 'other' categories, including victims of organ trafficking and those who are trafficked to be drug mules or fill other roles in organised crime syndicates (these do not qualify as labour trafficking since the entities they work for are not legally recognised).

These two broad categories – forced labour and sexual exploitation – each have countless subsets, as outlined by the US Department of State. Sexual exploitation runs the gamut from street prostitution to elite escort services where women and men are forced to engage in sexual activities with powerful people. Other varieties include forced pornography, where the victims are filmed and photographed, the most extreme form of which is snuff films, where the trafficked victim is killed for the thrill of paying customers. Trafficking for the purposes of forced marriage also falls under this broad heading.

Labour exploitation can be anything from children mining cobalt for batteries in the Congo, to impoverished women making designer coats below minimum wage in southern Italy, to enslaved people being forced to carry out cyber scams in South Asia. The subsets of labour trafficking are endless, and can include domestic workers like cleaners and carers, who work in plain sight and even live in the homes of their employers.

In the category labelled 'other', organ trafficking is a key area of concern, according to the Red Cross International Review. It does not, as one might first expect, involve the movement of organs after they are harvested. It involves the movement of unknowing victims whose kidneys, liver, lungs, or heart will save a wealthy patient, or whose corneas will give sight back to someone on a long organ donation waiting list. Organ trafficking occurs in major public and private hospitals from London to Los Angeles, and on battlefields from Ukraine to Syria.

Follow the money

At any given moment there are an estimated 16,000 migrants forced to sell sex on the streets of Europe, most of whom are from sub-Saharan Africa, according to the European Parliament. In the UK, one 2010 report estimated that approximately 2,600 people were trafficked for sex, of whom the majority were Chinese, according to the Association of Chief Police Officers (ACPO). In the US there are around 60,000 trafficking victims, the majority of whom are women trafficked for sex, according to DeliverFund.

On arrival in Italy, a trafficked Nigerian woman might 'owe' her trafficker around $30,000 for 'travel'. To earn the money to pay the trafficker, she has to work 12–14-hour days, during which she can charge up to $25 for intercourse, $15 for a blow job, and $5 for a hand job. If the client doesn't wear a condom, she can charge double. And she can charge more for anal sex or group sex, or if they want to film her. A 15-year-old trafficked girl can garner up to $50 on the streets of southern Europe for intercourse, and a 15-year-old boy can earn three times that.

The price structure is informal, but this is the street price in 2023, according to the rescued women at a shelter in Caserta run by sister Ruth. In a 12-hour day, the adult trafficking victim might make $300 if she turns a dozen tricks, or one an hour. She would have to work 1,000 days – nearly three years straight – earning $30 a day to make $30,000. But she also has to send money back home, pay around $25 a day to rent her space on the sidewalk, and around $500 a month for rent, clothes, beauty care and condoms. And how much did her trafficker really pay for her passage across the Mediterranean? The real sum is probably closer to around $7,000, leaving them with an estimated profit of $23,000.

The trafficking industry's influence is not confined to the streets, and not all of its proceeds are monetary. Human trafficking is generally thought to be an *underworld* crime associated with desperate poverty, which is exploited by mafias, organised crime syndicates, drug cartels, irregular migration and human smugglers. But the star-studded trafficking case of American financier Jeffrey Epstein, who was found hanging in his prison cell in a New York City federal jail in 2019, put trafficking on the map in a very different way. He and his British socialite accomplice Ghislaine Maxwell, who is currently serving a 20-year prison sentence in a minimum-security facility in the US state of Florida, were alleged to have recruited and paid girls as young as 14 for sex. When Epstein and his wealthy friends tired of them, Epstein and Maxwell then coerced them to recruit other girls their age. They are alleged to have pimped the girls out for cash and influence. Politicians, lawyers, entrepreneurs and even British royalty are all alleged to have used Epstein's private jet and visited his so-called 'paedophile island.' Even though names like former US president Bill Clinton and Prince Andrew have appeared on investigators' lists, none has been charged with crimes related to underage prostitution.

Epstein and Maxwell's case introduced the concept of trafficking to an audience beyond the small community of social workers, lawyers and journalists already well versed in one of the most prolific and least understood crimes against humanity. Many who followed Epstein's case had never considered trafficking could be a crime committed among the *upper world* elite. In her landmark book on the case, *Perversion of Justice*, Julie K. Brown painted a picture of how Epstein was able to get away with the crimes. 'He didn't do this alone,' she told National Public Radio

(NPR). 'He had a whole ecosystem that he created that allowed this to happen.'

As we will see, the same is true of all traffickers – they do not operate in isolation, but rely on wider networks. The ecosystems that enable trafficking in both upper and under worlds involve many parties and touch on other industries, from financial services to the travel industry.

Many of those who had been trafficked in Epstein's elite circle eventually came forward and won settlements from his estate. In underworld trafficking, most victims' best hope is survival. They will never be reimbursed for the sale of their bodies or their labour.

Meanwhile, the flow of money from these sales is gaining interest in big banks, according to a report by the Polaris project. In 2020, Deutsche Bank in New York and the Virgin Islands agreed to pay $150m in penalties for facilitating Epstein's sex trafficking. In 2023, they agreed to a further $75m settlement with the victims.

The bank is alleged to have turned a blind eye to more than $7m in payments involving individuals now publicly accused of being the buyers of Epstein's curated staple of elite sex-trafficked women. An additional $6m was paid through his accounts at the bank for legal fees, and $800,000 was paid to Russian and Eastern European models, to universities for tuition, and to hotels and other travel sector entities.

The settlements were just a fraction of what the bank earned in interest and transaction charges during Epstein's lengthy criminal career. 'In each of the cases that are being resolved today, Deutsche Bank failed to adequately monitor the activity of customers that the Bank itself deemed to be high risk. In the case of Jeffrey Epstein in particular, despite knowing Mr. Epstein's terrible criminal history, the Bank inexcusably failed to detect or prevent millions of dollars of suspicious transactions,' the Department of Financial Services of New York wrote in a statement.

A few weeks after Deutsche Bank settled, another big bank, JPMorgan, settled a similar suit tied to Epstein's sex trafficking charges, paying some $290m in penalties. Before banking at Deutsche Bank, Epstein kept hundreds of millions of dollars he earned under dubious circumstances at JPMorgan, which is thought to have collected $40m in fees through its relationship with Epstein.

Dozens of other banks and subsidiaries earned money from Epstein's criminal behaviour, ignoring red flags for the sake of millions in profits made both through Epstein and his clients who channelled money to him for the use of the girls he procured. Both banks and the subsidiaries they used to funnel money abroad and offshore knew full well of his 2008 conviction for procuring an underaged woman for the purpose of forced prostitution.

Deutsche Bank said in a statement, 'The settlement will allow dozens of survivors of Jeffrey Epstein to finally attempt to restore their faith in our system, knowing that all individuals and entities who facilitated Epstein's sex-trafficking operation will finally be held accountable.'

JPMorgan's statement was slightly more apologetic. 'The firm deeply regrets any association with this man, and would never have continued doing business with him if it believed he was using the bank in any way to commit his heinous crimes,' the firm said.

A way forward

The trafficking industry's profits are not just kept under mattresses or in locked safes in hideouts. They are kept in, and filtered through, some of the biggest and most powerful banks in the world, according to evidence given to a US Congress hearing. 'Follow the money and find the trafficker,' is an oft-quoted maxim in human trafficking circles, but it is an excruciatingly hard puzzle to crack, in part because financial institutions do everything they can to avoid closing the accounts of their biggest clients.

Anti-trafficking groups have long been pressurising big banks to stop turning a blind eye to shell accounts that allow traffickers to launder money unabated. Financial institutions, including the Vatican Bank, tend to offer low-interest deposit accounts that skirt rules as long as deposits stay under $10,000 a time, which is pocket change for most traffickers. Jackie Speier, a California representative in the US House, believes that banks have had a free pass for far too long. Attempts to require banks to flag activity that aligns with trafficking have largely been pushed back by the banking industry. She introduced legislation to impose minimum civil penalties on banks used by traffickers, making them liable both when they know their clients are involved in trafficking and when they protect them, which JPMorgan was fined for doing in the Epstein case. 'If banks are willing to be conduits for human trafficking, Congress should make it prohibitively expensive to do so,' she says. 'A banking license is not a free pass. It offers its holder a powerful privilege, which comes with the basic expectation to avoid funding crimes such as terrorism, the illegal drug trade, and human trafficking.'

Anti-trafficking groups like Polaris struggle to apply pressure to financial institutions to take stronger action in identifying accounts tied to traffickers, even when there are obvious indicators of money laundering. Banks sometimes argue they should not be required to play the role of law enforcement and that if they did so, they would put their employees at risk. Anti-trafficking advocates urge in-person bank employees to keep an eye out for suspicious activity like adults opening new accounts with a 'chaperone' accompanying them, or account holders who have no tax number or who deposit curious sums. Banks can be the gatekeepers, anti-trafficking groups say. But it will cost them the profits they would otherwise generate from these accounts.

Silvija Krupena, director of the London-based RedFlag Accelerator financial intelligence unit at RedCompass Labs, a consultancy that works with financial institutions to identify potential trafficking affiliations, blames banks for not doing enough. 'If banks embrace a data-driven, persona-based approach, they can reduce cost and increase investigation productivity and be more effective in their efforts to unmask perpetrators, strengthen prevention measures, and lead the charge against human trafficking,' she commented in a report quoted by Risk & Compliance Platform Europe.

Trafficking is a financial crime, but it is not treated like other criminal enterprises. Banks and financial institutions are required to play a major role in hunting out tax evaders, terrorists and money laundering tied to drug and arms trafficking. Yet they often give human traffickers a pass, according to a recent PriceWaterhouseCooper Consulting report on human trafficking in South East Asia.

Financial institutions are the only bodies that can find hidden money in their coffers (government and law enforcement agencies require search warrants and probable cause to search private accounts), and to do so, they must implement better protocols and algorithms to identify account holders who might be breaking the law. Meanwhile, as Krupena points out, traffickers continue to get smarter, bolder and more sophisticated in the means they use to launder money. 'Everyone can and must do more, but the financial sector is uniquely placed to disrupt human trafficking,' she writes. 'Financial data can reveal human crimes flowing through systems which are often hidden in plain view.'

So what are these fresh approaches banks and other financial institutions, especially those that operate virtually, need to do to help stop trafficking crimes? 'Traffickers have no borders, no budgets to consider and no data protection concerns,' Krupena says.

A 2020 *Compliance Week* survey among bank and financial institution employees found that 75 per cent are 'not confident' that they could spot human trafficking, yet the signs are there and with proper training they could be spotted. Instead, banks are reducing the amount of time spent face-to-face with clients and automating as much as possible. 'These challenges are worsened by an ineffective incentive model that promotes a 'box-ticking' compliance culture,' Krupena says.

Traffickers succeed by not getting caught, and they do that mostly by understanding the outer limits of the law and by not carrying out money laundering as flagrantly as other criminal enterprises, according to UNODC. A trafficker might easily and legally open dozens of accounts in different banks, funnelling money in small amounts to spread out their profits and avoid drawing suspicion.

In 2023, the Liechtenstein Initiative, a public–private partnership between the governments of Liechtenstein, Australia and the Netherlands and some private sector players, continues to update its five-point blueprint called FAST (Finance Against Slavery and Trafficking), established in 2019, to put banks at the heart of fighting human trafficking. The initiative, 'Blueprint for Mobilizing Finance Against Slavery and Trafficking', is directed at all financial sector actors, 'including banks, pension funds, insurers, fintech, regulators' and others who hold the key to taking action against modern slavery and human trafficking.

The five goals are:

- Increasing resources for financial investigations into modern slavery and human trafficking
- Developing better indicators of trafficking-related money laundering and terrorist financing risks
- Promoting collaboration across the sector on human rights due diligence and social risk mapping
- Developing detailed guidance which is a blanket policy for financial institutions to consider when reporting clients to law enforcement
- Investing in digital and social finance, including microfinance, to serve the most vulnerable.

Jessica Ramos, head of regulatory and oversight affairs at the European Women Payments Network, has worked to expose the role of banks' complicity in allowing those who make the most from the trade in humans to prosper unabetted. She said recently that the 'awkward truth is that numerous banks around the world are involved in processing the proceeds of modern slavery without being aware of the extent of the phenomenon or having the expertise to recognise and deal with it. The financial flows from these crimes move through the banking system allowing criminals to profit, expand their activities and further exploit vulnerable people.'

She has called for mandatory training to spot the signs of human trafficking, both for those frontline workers in the financial industry who deal with the public, and for those who process payments.

> There are many ... examples of observable contextual indicators, such as a customer making numerous cash deposits during off-peak hours, overnight or outside business hours; cash withdrawals in multiple cities at different times of day; frequent transportation and travel expenses not in line with the customer's stated business activity; multiple bank accounts opened for different customers using the same phone number, address and other data; an individual acting as controller of accounts for multiple unrelated individuals, payments to overseas employment agencies in high-risk countries that are inconsistent with business activity, or payroll accounts displaying unusual patterns, i.e. payroll expenditure is significantly lower than expected.

Anti-trafficking groups, including the Council of Europe's GRETA (Group of Experts on Action against Trafficking in Human Beings), Anti-Slavery International, and the UN Inter-Agency Coordination Group, have set up a clear and concise protocol for banks to consider, including identifying small cash deposits of round numbers and those made with large bills, and watching for those that happen out of business hours. Deposits in multiple cities are also a clue, since traffickers often control more than one victim using the same account.

The groups also say banks should look out for peer-to-peer payments for rounded increments. This could show that the payer is paying for something by the hour, whereas most peer-to-peer payments are for specific amounts. If an account receives a transfer for a rounded number and the same amount is quickly withdrawn, it can be a clue that traffickers are taking the money. Banks should also look for the same email address being used for multiple accounts.

The fact that some of these seemingly simple checks are not already being done consistently in an industry that turns more of a profit than many small countries helps to explain why trafficking continues to grow. An investigation by the International Consortium of Investigative Journalists in 2020 accused five major banks of ignoring blatant warning signs that their account holders were tied to illegal activities. 'The records show that five global banks – JPMorgan, HSBC, Standard Chartered Bank, Deutsche Bank and Bank of New York Mellon – kept profiting from powerful and dangerous players even after US authorities fined these financial institutions for earlier failures to stem flows of dirty money,' the group says. It pointed out that US agencies responsible for enforcing money laundering laws rarely prosecute megabanks. Ultimately, they say, the actions authorities do take 'barely ripple the flood of plundered money that washes through the international financial system'.

CHAPTER 2

GOING FOR BROKE

Brokers, smugglers and traffickers

It's 6pm in Paris, April 2015. A sophisticated-looking Middle Eastern man unbuttons his designer jacket before sinking into an overstuffed black leather chair at a cigar bar on the Champs-Élysées. Beads of sweat glisten on his temples as he settles into the quietest corner of the room, facing the wall. Two men on the other side of the bar are laughing over something they're sharing on an iPhone. A camel-coloured cashmere jacket hangs over another chair, but its owner is nowhere to be seen. Evening light filters through the heavy wooden blinds that cover the windows. The smoked mirrors lining the walls create the illusion that the bar is made up of small rooms.

A trace of cigar smoke permeates the room despite ventilation and neutralising cologne-scented candles. Everything is leather and dark wood, no soft textiles at all, but the aroma still lingers. The man stares ahead at nothing in particular for a long time, running through the figures in his mind, counting his losses. He picks up one of his phones and reads the news bulletin about the accident one more time, searching for clues that aren't there, because no one really knows exactly what happened. He puts his phone down again.

The waiter arrives with a bottle of $300 Courvoisier XO Royal cognac and pours a generous glass without asking the man what he wants to drink. He nods blankly and takes a sip. The waiter comes back with an ashtray and a leather box containing a lighter and cigar clip. The man pushes it away. A celebratory cigar will have to wait until he knows more.

The man is Mohamed El-Amin, one of the most successful media moguls in Egypt, the owner of 14 satellite channels and three newspapers, so he knows that news reporters are often wrong. He hopes they are wrong this time, too. He picks up his phone to search for any new updates that might have dropped.

'More than 900 feared dead,' he reads again. He can't understand why there were 900 people on one boat, the maths is all wrong. He had made it clear so many times that risks like this are just too costly. He hopes he wasn't fucked over again by greedy brokers and smugglers trying to save money.

He puts the phone down and looks around the room, thinking about all the deals he has made within these walls. His phone rings, but he doesn't answer it. He's not the only person who saw the headlines and is worried about the commodities lost at sea. So much money paid in advance, now all gone. If he can't deliver the girls who are now likely at the bottom of the Mediterranean Sea, he will have to find others to replace them, or pay back the buyers.

Notification of another news report pops up on his phone. The few survivors who managed to get plucked out of the Mediterranean by a merchant ship have told their rescuers that the boat departed from Libya and was headed for Italy. It doesn't tell him much. El-Amin knows that many people on the boats have no idea where they are embarking from, and details like that are surmised by journalists who make broad assumptions based on previous disasters. Most of the dead were locked below deck, he reads without emotion.

The scale of the disaster is notable, but the fact that it happened is hardly surprising. The central Mediterranean route used by people smugglers between Algeria, Egypt, Libya and Tunisia taking migrants to Italy and Malta is the most well-travelled and deadliest migrant route in the world, with nearly 29,000 people known to have died since 2014 trying to reach Europe, according to the IOM's Missing Migrants Project.

El-Amin calls his man in Italy. He should know by now if it is their boat. No answer. He turns off his caller ID and sends him an almost-blank message containing just ellipses, a signal he's more than a little concerned. Blame can be allocated later, punishments too, if necessary. Someone needs to pay for this mistake, for the greed that drove the costly decision to put his girls on the ill-fated ship.

He slowly finishes the cognac, checking his phone over and over for a message that finally comes.

'It wasn't ours,' his man in Italy writes, simply. 'Ours was picked up by the coastguard, they will arrive on the Italian main-land in four days.'

The man exhales deeply and motions the waiter over for another drink, and this time a cigar, too. He takes a Cuban out of the humidor the waiter sets on the table and cuts off the tip. He makes four calls to tell his most important clients the good news: their orders will be fulfilled soon, the girls will arrive. And the boy too, he tells one of his clients, don't worry.

In addition to his media empire, El-Amin runs a slew of elite orphanages from which his staff of women hand-pick young girls, and increasingly young boys, to be sold. They are moved across the North African coast to Libya, where they meld into the crowds of other people on the move. They are ear-tagged with coded earrings so the smugglers know they are a priority when they fill the boats. Older women often travel with them as chaperones, hoping to be rewarded with asylum despite having spent their lives exploiting young girls.

At a shelter in southern Italy, I once met an elderly woman who admitted escorting young Nigerian women destined for the forced sex industry and who described herself as 'converted'. She told me that the risk of dying crossing the sea was worth it, since women like her, essentially on-the-ground brokers, had little to lose. I was not entirely convinced she had changed her ways, and she was eventually kicked out of the shelter for trying to convince rescued sex trafficking victims to leave the shelter. Yet what she said stuck with me. She had risked her life to deliver victims to madams in Italy, yet she had no plan for herself once she got there.

In Egypt, some of the prettiest girls are held back for El-Amin himself. They can be sold later, his people have been told. The orphanage workers knew he prefers young virgins. In the past, virginity could be auctioned off along the migration trail to help offset the cost of the passage, but these days few girls make it to the boats without being raped. His staff insert IUDs or give them birth control pills to ration out. Sometimes the girls are steri-lised, which increases their street value, since it means they will more easily let the men who buy their sex have less need to use a condom, which garners almost double the price for the trick.

The biggest money in El-Amin's enterprise comes from the teenagers, but he still needs someone to bring them to his clients abroad, since he has no desire to get into the business of falsified documents. Anyway, there is really no need. It is much easier to just have the documents waiting for them in Italy when they arrive. Paying his man in Italy a small commission to produce each person's papers is a small price to pay to avoid the headache of such details. It's still a highly profitable business, and his media power protects him. For now.

When El-Amin was eventually arrested in 2022, it was because police had set up a sting operation that included surveilling the Parisian cigar bar. His conviction was for sexually assaulting and trafficking more than a dozen of the girls brought from his orphanage to his sweeping villa outside Cairo, but no one knows for sure how many of the girls in his institutions ended up being sent to Europe and sold into sexual slavery; the number is likely to be many times larger. El-Amin died in a private cancer hospital in Cairo in 2022, as reported by The New Arab, which he paid for despite having been sentenced to 26 years in prison.

* * *

The UN Refugee Agency (UNHCR) observed a spike in trafficking and smuggling across the Mediterranean Sea beginning from the Arab Spring in late 2010. At the outset of the Arab Spring, Libya was still a governed nation, albeit under Muammar Gaddafi's dictatorship. Back then, irregular migration was far more organised. Gaddafi, who ruled Libya's tribes and clans, often bragged that he controlled the flow of migration to Europe. The boats then were bigger and held more people but were not always safer.

Gaddafi used this power to strongarm European leaders like Italy's then-prime minister Silvio Berlusconi, who shared certain predilections with the Libyan leader. Neither drank, but both had a weakness for women. It was Gaddafi who is said to have introduced Berlusconi to the orgy-like 'bunga bunga' parties the prime minister often held in the basement of his Milan villa. This camaraderie wasn't limited to the bedroom; the *Financial Times* reported that Italy invested in Libya's infrastructure and oil production in exchange for a halt to migrant boat departures. There was even talk of building a pipeline under the Mediterranean Sea to ship Libyan oil into Europe. Those plans all stopped when Gaddafi was overthrown during the Arab Spring; he was killed on 10 October 2011 in a NATO-led attack on his convoy during the battle of Sirte. Since then, Libya has fallen into a largely lawless state with two governments trying to rule a population that trusts neither.

While Gaddafi was still alive, many of those on the boats were people from Libya, trying to escape the indiscriminate violence that comes from life under a dictatorship. But when Gaddafi's government fell, it paved the way for tribes and criminal gangs alike to profit from the smuggling of desperate people across the sea to Italy. Libya became a transit country, with some of its citizens making far more money exploiting migrants than they would ever make in Europe or beyond.

Since then, the facilitation of irregular migration from the shores of Libya has become a multi-million-dollar enterprise that has lined the pockets of certain Libyans. Very few Libyans are now among those who make the journey; instead, as the Global Detention Project reports, widespread corruption and political chaos has allowed the country to become a major transit country where tens of thousands of migrants get caught and wait until someone pays to free them so they can continue their journey.

The exodus of refugees produced by the Arab Spring drove the creation of new migration routes and smuggling methods which were ripe for use by the trafficking industry. According to the Global Compact for Migration Objectives, militias and tribes started vying for desperate people, sometimes buying and selling them through brokers to keep the boats as full as possible, as revealed in IOM surveys.

* * *

Many smugglers operate on the dark web, where they can be found by anyone searching for transit to Europe. Of course, the smugglers don't call themselves that. Instead, their ads say they are in the business of 'realising opportunities,' and are filled with Tripadvisor-style reviews that, like those for many seedy hotels, seem to mostly be fake. Some ads describe the voyage across the Mediterranean Sea like a cruise, with supposed 'clients' and 'passengers' describing the ease with which they found work and integrated once they arrived, a demonstrable lie.

Some of the groups don't even bother to go very far underground, instead using closed groups on Facebook and Telegram to advertise. One advertisement on Facebook, placed by someone going by the name Abdul Aziz, and found by the BBC, read, 'With the beginning of the new season we have a range of journeys on offer. Turkey Libya Italy, $3,800. Algeria Libya Italy, $2,500. Sudan Libya Italy, $2,500 ... The boats are all wood ... If you have questions, contact me on Viber or WhatsApp.' (But once potential clients bite, there are surcharges and extras, including the cost of lodging while the boats are prepared, which usually pushes the total fee up to around $7,000.) Aziz claimed to have 'agents' in 'almost every Arab state' and even sweetened the deal, saying 'kids go free' and offering to help if getting to Libya was too difficult. 'If people can't get here to Libya, I have legal and illegal ways to get them into the country.' The ad was taken down after an Interpol investigation.

One smuggler I met described the sale of human beings as if he were running a travel agency, saying he made sure all the seats on his tours were taken to keep overheads down. In reality, empty boats are a cost the smuggler never accepts. It is simply better to delay a departure than send a boat half full.

Some advertise false documents. 'Travelling straight to Europe by plane costs between €4,000 and €8,000. If you only want a passport and pay for the plane ticket yourself, and you take the consequences, then the price is €4,000 for a 100% genuine passport belonging to someone who looks like you,' one advertisement promises. The advert quickly segues from smuggling into trafficking: 'But if you want to pay after arriving in Europe, the price is €8,000 and we will pay for everything and take all the risk. Just send your picture and your number via Facebook message so we can find a passport belonging to someone who looks like you, and then we will call you.'

By far the most common promise on smugglers' ads, both on the dark web and in mainstream social media, are those promising that NGO charity boats or Italian military rescue ships will save the passengers. One shows a map of the perilous sea between Libya and Italy with a red dot. 'The big red dot in the middle of the sea is a European Red Cross ship which helps refugees and takes them directly to Italy, after giving them permission to leave Italy legally,' the ad states, in a promise that is both a horrible distortion and frighteningly close to the truth.

Traffickers recruit from those who express interest in these sites, but who can't afford to pay the hefty prices for passage. If someone writes to express interest and then doesn't follow up, many of the smugglers will send on their contacts to brokers, who then work with the traffickers to see if a deal can be cut. If the person is a young man or woman, the traffickers are often happy to help. There is less appetite to help couples with children, unless the children can be exploited in some way.

Finding recruits is easy. After all, for those escaping poverty and war, coming up with several thousand euros in cash is often impossible, making the most desperate the easiest targets for exploitation. In many cases, those who succumb would qualify for asylum under UN protocols, but there are few opportunities to apply for such asylum in the countries they are fleeing from, giving them no choice but to try to make it on their own.

Once someone who can't afford the smuggler's passage prices takes the bait, the traffickers own them. What starts as gratitude to their traffickers soon turns to anger once they realise how much they owe, and despair at what they have to do to pay it back. Assuming they survive the trip.

* * *

Soon after Gaddafi fell, militia members found their way into Libya's armed services, which continued to function under both of the country's parallel governments. The Libyan coastguard, which runs under the armed services, is funded by the European Union through Italy, which donates boats and offers training.

But the Libyans have been shown to use quite different methods, including shooting at NGO rescue vessels and refusing to hand out life jackets to migrants on overcrowded ships. If a few passengers fall in, and they often do, little effort is made to retrieve them. Countless videos by NGO rescue vessels intercepted by the Libyan coastguard demonstrate horrific acts of human rights abuses, including one incident when a migrant who fell off during a transfer to the rescue vessel was dragged in the sea until his lifeless body slipped under the water. Other migrants who have been rescued have gunshot wounds they say were caused by Libyans on previous 'rescue' operations. It's a far cry from the 'effective, humanitarian and safe' migration and asylum policy which the EU claims it is developing.

When the Libyan coastguard, and more recently the Tunisian coastguard, stop migrant boats at sea before they can be rescued, they are essentially recycling the migrants and refugees, who are carted back to detention centres and re-exploited, re-prostituted and forced to return to labour work in oilfields and elsewhere until they raise enough money to pay for another ticket for passage. The fee is usually paid to a relative or associate of a Libyan coastguard member. For those trafficked people who get pushed back, the stakes are higher since they will now owe their traffickers twice the money for passage.

Bright's story

In early 2024, I met an 18-year-old from Ghana who called himself Bright. He was begging in front of the grocery store near my apartment in central Rome. His dream was to go to England and open a street food stall. Despite having been in Italy for more than six months when I started talking to him, he felt he was just starting his journey. But things were not going according to plan.

He had begun by making his way to Agadez, Niger, a hub for irregular migration where, as Migrant Media Network discovered, those with money can find someone to drive them to the Libyan border, and those without will be easily found by traffickers. Bright was smart, but low on cash after being robbed by people travelling with him. In Agadez he met another man from Ghana who – kindly, he thought – lent him the money to get to Libya, then to Italy. As he told the story, I could guess what happened next.

In retrospect, he now doesn't even believe the man was from his home country. But at the time he was tired, broke and scared. He was younger than many travellers, and the man seemed like a father figure. He gave Bright a mobile phone and lent him the money using the hawala system, which the International Monetary Fund (IMF) describes as an informal way to move money without physically transferring it. This method of finance is called various names depending on the country (fei-ch'ien ('flying money') in China, padala in the Philippines, hundi in India, hui kuan in Hong Kong, phei kwan in Thailand), but generally refers to an untraceable network of money transfers made from one location to another through service providers known as hawaladars. The system has been in use since at least the 14th century, and was the cornerstone of ancient trade at a time when it was dangerous to travel carrying gold. In some places with limited financial services it is still popular for everyday transactions, but today it is also widely used by terrorists and traffickers, according to the IMF. The International Centre for Counter-Terrorism reports that the FBI found it was even used to fund the 9/11 terrorists.

At its most basic level, a network of hawaladars in different countries transfer money using a series of promises and codewords. Bright's trafficker in Agadez paid a local hawaladar a sum close to $15,000 on his behalf to cover the smuggling costs from Niger to Italy, and then Italy to the UK. Bright knew he would have to pay it back, but his trafficker assured him he would work along the way and be able to pay it off in small tranches to various hawaladars. Bright's story underscores the point at which smuggling becomes trafficking. Because he did not have his own money to pay the smuggler for his journey, a trafficker preyed on him and offered to pay the travel expense for him, knowing they could eventually force him to work for very little money and under difficult circumstances. Desperate, he agreed to take the 'loan' that indebted him to his trafficker.

The trafficker paid the smuggler directly in Agadez, and also paid an Agadez hawaladar to transfer money to Libya. The money was picked up by an associated hawaladar in Libya, who took care of the cost of putting Bright on a boat to Italy. Once in Italy, Bright was meant to meet a broker who was tied to the Neapolitan Camorra crime syndicate near Naples.

Because Bright was under 18 at the time, when he arrived in Italy he was placed in an asylum centre for unaccompanied minors. His traffickers infiltrated the centre and tried to recruit him to act as a drug runner for the Camorra using an 'assistant'. Italian law enforcement officials explained to me that these assistants are generally other migrants who stay inside the centres but work for traffickers.

Bright immediately resisted and went to the authorities. Because of his age, and because at the time Italy was governed by a left-wing government that had allowed more people to be given asylum, he was given protection.

Before Brexit, the asylum papers Bright got in Italy might have been enough to move on to the UK, but not under the current post-Brexit immigration scheme. The last time I talked to Bright, his plan was to use his legal papers to get to France and then cross to the UK however he could, which would almost certainly be illegally.

He explained that he had already met a man—likely a broker—who had promised him help. When I asked if he was worried about falling into another trafficker's trap, he said he would still risk anything to get to England. 'This was my plan,' he told me. 'I have to try any way I can. I left everything for this, and if it kills me to get there, so be it.'

* * *

Mr El-Amin's man in Italy was a man I will call Joey, because of his resemblance to the *Friends* character. We are sitting in his office when he tells me the story of the boat that sank with 900 people on board, and the arrest of his former boss in Paris a year earlier, and how both incidents nearly put him out of business. The horrific accident that made headlines around the world in 2015 shook up a lot of people in his line of work. There was a moment when they all thought their inventory might have gone down with the ship. Joey says he did lose nearly a dozen people in the disaster, people he was transporting for other clients. He does not condone the overcrowding of ships like that.

'Too many people on board, it was a breach of contract,' he tells me. 'The maximum is always five hundred or less, more than that is just too risky.'

The Venetian-style metal blinds over the only window in Joey's ground floor office are bent ever so slightly, just enough to steal a glance outside without moving them. The room reeks of stale Toscano cigar smoke – it's a far cry from the cigar bar in Paris – and is anything but luxurious, even though it has some of the same characteristics. A worn leather chair in the corner and a small table with a stained ashtray. A leather footstool in front of it has been repaired with duct tape so many times, it is hard to see what colour the leather once was. Million-dollar deals go down in this hovel all the time. But the money never arrives here. It is counted in the plush corner offices in the world's biggest banks and financial institutions, where it is easily laundered.

A smell lingers in this room, too, but not of expensive Cuban cigars. It's an odour of unwashed bodies, though it is not coming from Joey, who is sitting behind the desk in front of me. Joey smells of the sort of musk-based cologne that was popular in the 1980s. The smell in the room is the kind that lingers in air that doesn't circulate. The window is never opened, even briefly. Bars that would normally be on the outside are embedded into the glass, so even if it breaks, no one can get in – or out.

Joey's clothes are clean and ironed, and his fingernails freshly manicured, complete with what looks like transparent gloss. He is wearing pristine New Balance trainers and striped socks. Three chargers attached to three iPhones of different vintages are lined up neatly on the scratched top of an army green desk that still has an American flag decal on the side, an artefact saved from a land-fill that came from one of the seven US bases that dot Italy.

The only other thing on the desk is another stained ashtray for the cheap cigars Joey lights with a bright blue lighter on which the word 'Italia' is written in white, and which he chain smokes as we speak. Nothing hangs on the walls, though nails protrude as if in a previous incarnation the office was decorated with diplomas or awards.

Joey's face is scarred from what I first thought was acne, but later learned was a fiery car accident. He describes his survival as some sort of heroic event, rather than the criminal escape it probably was. It was when he was younger, he says, showing me the skin grafts on his arms that had once been covered with tattoos. One remaining tattoo looks like a poster that has been partially torn off a wall.

It is hard to guess Joey's age. His hair is dyed jet black. His eyebrows show a hint of auburn, his face is puffy and his cheeks hairless, likely from some aesthetic procedure that unsuccessfully tried to smooth out the burn scars. He wears a flat-faced pinkie ring on his left hand that would leave a spectacular bruise if he hit someone squarely. His tan is too even, as if it is either sprayed on or from a tanning bed. Despite the manicure, his muscular hands are those of a worker, someone who has hammered nails or moved bricks, or maybe even dug graves. He has not had this desk job his whole life. But whatever he did to move up the ranks to where he is now, he feels he deserves his position of power. It's easy to imagine him sitting in the overstuffed leather chair in the corner, feet up, dreaming of his own ascent. But for now, there are clearly many layers to the hierarchy above him.

Whenever one of the phones rings, he signals with a dismissive sweeping motion for me to leave the room and sit on the worn-out brown leather sofa in the hallway outside his office, from which I can see a tiny kitchen with a very dirty sink and a one-burner hob on which rests a silver moka coffee maker. What appears to be a bathroom is behind another door down the dark hallway to the left, but given the state of the kitchen, I am not tempted to investigate further.

To the right is a thick bulletproof door with multiple locks. A tiny black and white monitor is attached to the wall beside the door. At first I assume it shows who is outside. I see a group of young men in the monitor at one point, but they do not ring any doorbell that I can hear. Later, I deduce that there is no surveillance camera outside that door; the CCTV must be monitoring something else.

The door to Joey's office is also reinforced, but the security locks are on the outside of the door, allowing someone to be locked inside. A hatch in the ceiling leads to some unseen crawl space, or perhaps an escape route. When I eventually leave, I see on the outside of the office the scars of several attempts to break in.

Sitting in the hallway, I can hear Joey speak in hushed Arabic. On another call, he speaks French, and on another Italian, which is the language we use, even though neither of us is a native speaker. On the calls he rattles off amounts of money in various currencies, almost like an auctioneer. Sometimes he hangs up abruptly.

When he finishes each call, he opens the door and returns to his seat behind the desk. He doesn't invite me to come back in, but he doesn't tell me not to either, so I return each time until he eventually tells me I should leave because he has someone coming for a meeting. After I leave, I wait for more than an hour down the street to see who he might be meeting. No one arrives, at least not through the door I left from.

We are in a coastal town on the Italian mainland just a few miles from some of the most expensive beachfront property in Europe. This is the heart of organised crime country, near a port that often serves as an arrival point for migrants saved at sea, but that is all I can divulge. The meeting hinged on a promise of complete anonymity to Joey, who considers himself a migrant 'assistant' who 'facilitates' the arrival of 'clients' for whom his 'partners' in Libya, and more recently Tunisia, arrange 'tickets' for passage to Italy.

'They need me,' he says of his clients. 'I help them.'

There are thousands of broker Joeys in the complicated world of human trafficking. They are the key middlemen who link the traffickers and the smugglers at each end of the trade in human bodies. But brokers are expendable and easily replaceable for both groups. Joey's arrest, or his murder for a mistake that cost the traffickers too much money, would probably have no lasting impact on their multi-billion-dollar enterprise.

Brokers like Joey often start out as smugglers; maybe he had his own network of men who could procure decommissioned boats and their engines, or who could construct the massive rubber dinghies which have become such an integral aspect of people smuggling.

The dinghies are specially made – no camping store sells dinghies with capacity for hundreds of people. They are easily hidden under sand on the beaches of North Africa from the authorities and competing smuggling rings. They are an economical alternative to the more traditional massive blue fishing boats that can hold many hundreds of desperate, lucrative human cargo. But the dinghies are too flimsy to make it all the way to Italy. They rely on there being an intermediary salvor along the way, either a merchant ship, an NGO rescue vessel, the Italian coastguard or navy, or the European border control Frontex fleet. Sometimes they are pushed back by the Libyan and Tunisian coastguards.

Countless people who have been rescued from the dinghies have told stories of being forced on to them at gunpoint after pleading not to be sent across the sea on something so dangerous. When the smugglers have enough people to send out, they half-inflate the dinghies and then instruct the women and children to sit on planks of wood in the flat centre and make the men straddle the edges while they finish inflating. That's the only way to ensure that those sitting in the centre are packed tightly enough not to move and cause the boat to capsize. The men, with one leg inside and one leg outside, keep the craft balanced, but they also can't easily move. Sometimes the wooden planks in the centre break, which causes the dinghy to buckle. Or something punctures the thick rubber, and the boat deflates and sinks.

The Italian coastguard and other rescuers generally burn the dinghies once the people are taken to safety. NGO rescue teams mark the dinghies with the date and number of people rescued, and leave the vessels at sea. If there are still engines on board, smugglers will come and fetch them. But fishermen and merchant ship crews often spot the deflated boats at sea with no markings, and there is no way to know if their passengers were rescued or drowned.

Working as a middleman, or broker, like Joey, is a step up to being the kingpin of one's own trafficking ring. The kingpin is the one who makes the real money, the one who controls the flow of bodies based on what the market needs – whether prostitutes, drug mules or healthy kidneys. But the kingpin needs men like Joey who can find them all.

In Italy, traffickers and brokers are often part of the same organised crime syndicates, or loosely tied criminal gangs, though the roles are entirely different. The top end deals with procuring transportation for the movement of trafficked people and the bottom end deals with providing it.

* * *

No one pocketing the real profits from the smuggling business ever boards a ship or crawls into the dark trailer of a long-haul truck beside their human cargo. There are plenty of people lower in the hierarchy of the industry to do it for them.

In sea-borne smuggling, the criminal groups usually coerce a migrant to do the dirty work, which then puts them – not the smuggler or trafficker – at risk of arrest if they are caught. Would-be migrants who have seafaring experience are asked to captain the vessels, according to testimony given by those migrants facing trial as smugglers. Often they pay nothing, or a fraction of the fee, if they take command. But they are also frequently not given a choice.

In 2023, the Italian movie *Io Capitano*, which was nominated for a Golden Globe and an Academy Award in the foreign film category in 2024, traced the true story of teenage Senegalese cousins who travelled to Libya to cross the sea, paying their life savings for the crossing. The smugglers offered Mamadou Kouassi Pli Adama, known as Mama, a discounted fare to drive the ship, which he and his severely injured cousin did, to safety. The smugglers who sold the passage to the young men suggested that if he drove the boat, being just 16, he would likely not face prosecution due to his age. Mama didn't understand at the time, and on arrival was unabashedly proud of helping get the overcrowded boat safely to shore. Thinking he would be applauded for his heroics, Mama admitted he was the captain, unaware that he had unwittingly confessed to being what the Italian authorities would consider a smuggler.

I interviewed Mama at the Venice Film Festival, where *Io Capitano* debuted. Now in his forties, he tells the story of so many people like him. 'I survived threats in Senegal, torture in Libya, and persecution in Italy,' he says. Now he is an activist for a cooperative that helps young men like him. He described the mindset that drives many would-be migrants into the hands of traffickers: 'Once you decide to go, you no longer have alternatives. You just willingly set off on the dangerous journey where you don't know if you'll stay alive.' Today he has a partner, two children, and residency rights in Italy, but he spoke about the long struggle that awaits those who do survive and make it to Europe, and the difficulty of obtaining a residence permit and 'being able to live a dignified life'.

Mama is a typical example of how, time and again, migrants are scapegoated to satisfy the public's calls to stop smuggling rings, even though in almost every case, the smugglers and traffickers who are profiting are nowhere near the boats. Authorities turn a blind eye to the fact that the person driving the boat is never arrested with pockets of cash, a detail also largely overlooked in headlines. The only times when cash is sequestered as part of breaking up a trafficking ring is when the arrests are made on dry land – or by freezing assets held in financial institutions.

Sometimes there are contradictory reports that make it hard to tell who is a smuggler and who is being smuggled, but generally, authorities will identify those who are driving the boats or are on the top deck, not locked in the hulls below.

Only 27 people survived the April 2015 shipwreck which the Egyptian media mogul and Joey were so worried about. More than 800 people died. A 28-year-old Tunisian man named Mohammed Ali Malek was eventually convicted and sentenced to 18 years in prison under Italy's anti-trafficking laws for driving the boat. His lawyers called him a scapegoat, but many of the survivors said he was also the person who ferried them in smaller dinghies to the larger vessel about a mile off the Libyan coast the day the ill-fated ship set sail. He was also reportedly milling around the illegal centre where money was paid to the smuggling ring for the crossing, though his lawyer told me that he was there, like everyone else, to buy passage. He didn't have any money on him at the time of his arrest, nor in his bank account in Tunisia.

One theory Italian authorities put forth in court was that he knew that, as a Tunisian, he would be deported back to Tunisia, so driving the vessel over was easy money, and he was ensured a free ticket back home. But his wife and their two-year-old child had actually made it across the sea to Italy in late 2014, and his lawyer insisted he was crossing to join them, and that because he had experience on fishing vessels, he was given a discount to act as the ship's skipper. The signs seem to indicate that he may have been part of the smuggling ring, but he was definitely not a high-level trafficker, even though that's why he's in jail.

I got Joey's number from an NGO rescue ship worker who sometimes passed it on to rescued people in need of someone to help them on the ground. Joey agreed to meet me under a false premise. I told him I was trying to find a lost relative from Afghanistan, who I claimed had been in possession of his phone number when she had recently arrived in Italy by boat. It was a distorted version of my great-grandmother's story, and although it was fabricated, I'm sure that I still have blood relatives in Afghanistan. It is entirely possible that they may have tried to leave via the very migrant trail I was investigating.

I originally told Joey I had lost track of my cousin and that she wasn't in any refugee centre. I asked if he could help me track her down. He said that he could do some checking. If he found her and had to 'remove' her from wherever she was, I would have to pay around $1,500, but he could do a few checks for free.

I don't feel particularly bad about lying to Joey. I don't know his real name and I have no idea which of the three iPhones I called to reach him is his, or how often he changes SIMs. The only thing I do know with certainty is where I met him, in that strange, centrally located office. I have no doubt the police knew him, what he did, and who he worked for. That is not to say Italy officially condones human trafficking or people smuggling, but there is little done here to stop the movement of people onward, very much as Mexico does little to stop people trying to enter the US or France tries to stop people leaving Calais. Italy is not, by definition, a transit country like Libya and Tunisia, but in practice that is exactly what happens in many cases of trafficking, except when the final destination of the victims is forced sex work on Italian back roads or forced labour in the agriculture and fashion industries.

After I first reached out to Joey, he called me back on Telegram to ask me if I was a journalist. I admitted the truth, and he didn't seem at all bothered. He agreed to meet me anyway. He simply insisted I never disclose where we met. 'A lot of people don't understand that what we are doing is helping the migrants find their future,' he said. He saw himself as a sort of Robin Hood-style saviour. And even though his work potentially sends hundreds of people into far worse situations than those they left behind, he is absolutely right about helping them find their futures, bleak as they may be. As for those who make it through the labyrinth and do actually find better lives, they also couldn't have done it without people like him.

Joey insists that he doesn't pocket a lot of money. 'The real money goes north,' he says, referring to complicit financial organisations who enable the laundering of money made on trafficking people. 'Brussels and Geneva ... they are the ones who line their pockets.'

Joey explains that almost no one who comes to Italy wants to stay here. 'They all want to go to England,' he says, laughing.

'Such fools. No one speaks English and no one even knows the UK isn't part of Europe any more, but they still want to go.'

A way forward

In 2023, when the political situation in Tunisia collapsed, thousands of smuggler boats made it to the Italian island of Lampedusa unassisted and unfettered. Despite calls from the European Union for the Tunisian government to throw money at breaking up the trafficking and smuggling rings in Tunisia, nothing stopped the boats. A whole new slew of ads from Tunisian brokers started popping up on Facebook, Telegram and underground networks – until late summer, when Tunisia accepted money and started taking migrants waiting to cross the sea to the desert border with Libya.

Stopping brokers like Joey and trafficking kingpins like Mohamed El-Amin is complicated by a lack of legal compliance at the most basic level, especially in destination countries.

The US State Department identifies Italy, one of the wealthiest countries in the world, as a Tier 2 country when it comes to battling trafficking because the government 'does not fully meet the minimum standards for the elimination of trafficking'. In Italy, which, according to the Council on Foreign Relations, is now the main gateway country for irregular immigration into Europe, investigations into trafficking are carried out by anti-mafia police units. They tend to focus on the ties between traffickers and criminal organisations – of which the country has an abundance – over rescuing victims.

Despite some successful prosecutions, Italy never compensates trafficking victims, and often expels them unless they can be taken in by charity groups such as those run by the Catholic

Church. Funding for victim programmes is often earmarked, but rarely delivered, according to a recent report by GRETA, which noted a decrease in both investigations and compensation. 'Even if compensation is granted by courts to victims participating as a civil party in criminal proceedings, it can take several years before the final decision,' the group says, also noting their concern that 'no victims of trafficking have received compensation from the fund for anti-trafficking measures.'

The primary complaints by NGOs and other groups working with the Italian government to try to stop trafficking is that the entities within the Italian civil service sector that are designed to help are short-staffed, under-funded and lack motivation to truly help the victims of all forms of trafficking. After the election of the right-wing government under Giorgia Meloni in 2022, programmes for victims deteriorated even more, with funds meant for anti-trafficking projects diverted to the building of detention centres for deporting migrants, whose arrivals topped 157,000 for the year. Deportations for the same year were fewer than 5,000, according to Italy's Interior Ministry. The backlog for processing asylum requests in Italy is more than two years, according to the government, meaning that many people move on before their cases are heard. If they miss a hearing, they are issued an expulsion order in absentia, which means if they try to enter the country at a later date, they will be denied entry or risk incarceration.

* * *

A young Nigerian woman who was under the thumb of her trafficker used to sell her body not far from the Baths of Caracalla in central Rome day in, day out, whatever the weather. One day I interviewed her, trying to find out more about why she didn't flee.

Miriam, as she told me her name was, said she had tried endlessly to leave, and had even called a helpline number multiple times, but the helpline only functioned during certain hours of the day and every time she tried to call, she was put on hold for hours. She could not afford to stop working during the time it would take to wait, so I offered to call the helpline for her the next day. I was on hold for 90 minutes, and when an operator answered, I explained the situation and said Miriam needed help. I gave the address where she could be found, and said she had tried to call on her own. The operator informed me that I could not call on her behalf, and even if Miriam got through, they could only put her on a waiting list since all the beds allotted for trafficking victims in Rome's shelters were full. I went back to tell Miriam to keep trying to call, and to get her name on a waiting list for a bed in a shelter. I suggested she go to the police, too, but she said she had tried and they had only told her to call the helpline.

A few months later, Miriam disappeared from her usual spot. I called the mobile phone number she had given me. A different woman answered the phone and when I asked to speak to Miriam, she said she had no idea who Miriam was.

This is the reality of getting help in most of Europe. Helplines that do exist are not efficient. Shelters are small, the number of beds allocated to victims far too few, and protections practically non-existent. There are thousands of Miriams on the streets of Europe who desperately want to be saved. There just isn't the will to save them.

Follow the money

A 2005 study by the ILO estimated that the global profits made by 'agents and brokers' (interchangeable roles depending on the countries in which they are identified and arrested) who managed the world's 9.8 million people forced into labour – from sweatshops to harvest crews to domestic servitude – pocketed around $44.3bn a year. That number boiled down to around $4,500 per victim annually. The ILO said the largest profits of this type of trafficking are made in industrial nations. Corrupt agents and brokers in the US made $18.8bn, those in Asia $13.7bn, those in Latin America $5.7bn. By contrast, agents in transit countries like Libya and Tunisia on the route to Europe, and France and the Balkans on the route to the UK pocket some $3.6bn, according to ILO figures. The lowest profits are the Middle East and North Africa, where corrupt agents only make around $3.6bn, and sub-Saharan Africa, where they make less than a billion, in part because in those regions the governments may well be part of the trafficking mechanism, and therefore impossible to trace.

A huge proportion of irregular migrants are trafficked – one 2016 survey by the IOM, reported in *The Guardian*, found that around 70 per cent of those arriving in Europe by sea having travelled overland through Africa each year had been trafficked at some point on the journey. Joey's profits are based on what the traffickers are willing to pay, a sum which is set by demand, as recounted by thousands of people who are rescued at sea. By way of example, consider that a trafficker dealing in sex slaves in Europe pays a broker like Joey the 2024 going rate (according to the IOM) of $10,000 apiece for ten Nigerian women who have already arrived in Libya – a sum of $100,000.

Joey then has to pay the smuggler $7,000 a person, or whatever deal he can cut on a bulk human cargo shipment, to get the women to Europe. He can often lower the per-person price if he has a group of ten and if he pays in cash instead of using the hawala system. Assuming he was able to cut a deal for $60,000 for ten people ($1,000 discount per person as a bulk rate), Joey has pocketed $40,000 for the ten women, and the smuggling ring has made $60,000.

But there are always incidental losses along the way, like accidental death or suicide. If Joey loses one woman on the way, he will then owe the trafficker $10,000, which will most likely be redeemed in the next deal. The broker incurs the loss rather than the trafficker because he did not effectively deliver his promised shipment of ten women. After all, it was up to him to choose the right smuggler to ensure the commodity was delivered.

Even though the price paid is for travel all the way from a home country or transit point to Europe, the journey is far from direct, which means the broker often has to shell out another $1,000 or more per person to pay off guards and get his charges out of detention centres in Libya or Tunisia, and a few hundred dollars more to hide them in a safe house until a smuggler can arrange a boat with enough paying people to make it worth sailing. Often, brokers team up with smugglers, which brings them discounts, favours to call in, and other ways to increase their profit margins without impacting the profit of the trafficker.

Under this scheme, the broker can guarantee a profit of between $2,500 and $3,000 a person. The smuggler makes his negotiated $6,000 per person for passage, the guards pocket their bribe money, the person who runs the safe house pockets his or her share. But the trafficker's upfront investment of $10,000 could triple or even quadruple by the time the ten Nigerian women work off their debt bondage, which can range from $30,000 to $50,000 a person depending on where they end up.

In the best-case scenario, if the ten Nigerian women make it across the sea alive, the trafficker could easily pull a profit of $300,000 on a $100,000 investment, the smuggler will have made $60,000 off the women, whether or not the boat makes it across, and the broker will have made $30,000 for doing the least risky work. And this is just for ten trafficked people. In 2023 alone, more than 157,000 people of whom 70 per cent, or 110,000, were likely trafficked, entered Italy – if those people made the traffickers even half the median, that's more than $50bn in a single year for traffickers who work the central Mediterranean route.

But if the boat goes down, or the women are taken to shelters for trafficking victims, which rarely happens, the trafficker loses his initial investment of $100,000. The broker and the smuggler and the safe house owner will still all profit, though the trafficker might pay less the next time he uses Joey's services. When boats go down, the traffickers are the biggest losers. That is after, of course, the women who lost their lives. Although it seems that they are the last thing on anyone's mind.

CHAPTER 3

BLOOD MONEY

Life and death at sea

Expensive yachts ply the turquoise waters of the Mediterranean Sea all summer long, their passengers disembarking only to eat at Michelin-starred restaurants and drink cocktails at sunset. On board, linen-clad passengers are waited on by white-gloved stewards, and the days are spent snorkelling, swimming and whiling away the hours sunbathing. Below deck, a chef prepares the meals and a cleaning crew quietly tidies up throughout the day and washes down the yacht thoroughly each night as the guests sleep.

Even the small yachts are worth millions of dollars. But luxury vessels aren't the only valuable boats at sea. Worth more than many of the yachts are decommissioned North African fishing vessels with peeling blue paint and rotting wooden hulls. Even massive rubber dinghies are worth more than $1m. Below decks on the wooden boats, there are no chefs; instead, migrant and refugee women and children are packed in tight, unable to move – the hatch is locked to avoid upsetting the delicate balance that keeps the rickety ship afloat with so many people on board. Those on the massive rubber dinghies sit in puddles of gasoline or straddle the sides, their feet dangling in the cold water. There are no bathrooms. Instead, the passengers often don't eat or drink anything days before they leave, to avoid having to use a toilet.

In July 2013, Italian entrepreneur Regina (Rita) Egle Liotta Catrambone and her American husband Christopher Catrambone were sailing off the shores of Malta in a luxury yacht when Rita noticed something floating in the water in the distance. As she looked through her binoculars, she realised it was a winter coat, not something you'd expect to see in the turquoise waters of the Mediterranean Sea at the height of summer.

She summoned the captain of their sleek vessel, who explained that it was likely from a migrant ship that went down during the spring, sending 368 people to an aquatic grave. No survivors had been found, and the only reason anyone in Europe knew the boat existed is because it had sent out a distress call before disappearing.

Debris from migrant boats – including water bottles, life jackets, and even broken boat pieces – were, at the time, becoming an inconvenience for holidaymakers on yachts sailing between Malta and Italy. The growing number of boats was also becoming a problem. According to maritime law, anyone on a vessel must 'render assistance' to anyone in distress; and every state should immediately search for boats making distress calls within their search and rescue (SAR) zones. Maritime law specifically states that such assistance should be based on non-discrimination of those in need of help, whether it be an enemy in time of war, or a migrant ship in territorial waters. Yet Malta, which is closer than Italy to the North African coast, where boats leave, has (according to a report by the European Council on Refugees and Exiles (ECRE)) been sanctioned for ignoring distress calls, leaving the Italian authorities to patrol much of the Central Mediterranean SAR zone.

Merchant ships often pass within metres of boats in distress without stopping, and fishermen often steer away. They have good reason to do so, since bringing rescued migrants to shore has been prosecuted under Italian law as abetting illegal immigration. In 2007, the *Belfast Telegraph* reported that seven Tunisian fishermen who had rescued 44 migrants off the coast of Tunisia and brought them to Lampedusa faced 15 years in prison for rescuing them, which set an alarming precedent for many locals. Again in 2018, six Tunisian fishermen were charged for the same act, but this time the Tunisian Fishermen Association of Zarzis sent a letter to the Italian embassy in Tunis to protest. 'Captain Bourassine and his crew are hardworking fishermen whose human values exceed the risks they face every day,' it said. 'When we meet boats in distress at sea, we do not think about their colour or their religion.'

I interviewed a fisherman in Lampedusa in the summer of 2023 who told me about how he and his colleagues frequently pulled up skulls and even whole bodies in their nets from migrant boat wrecks. He throws them back into the water. 'It's too risky to bring them to shore,' he told me at the dock. 'It's a much more dignified death to just be thrown back to sea.' The fishermen in Lampedusa and Tunisia avoid migrant boats at all costs. 'Even if we escape being charged [by Italian authorities] for following maritime law, they will sequester our boats for months, or even years, to investigate. It's not worth it.'

Captains of private yachts often do the same thing when they spot a migrant ship packed with people on the horizon. Sometimes they sail miles out of the way to avoid the terrible dilemma: rescue the passengers and risk being accused of abetting illegal immigration, or ignore the desperate people. In June 2024, CNN reported that the Spanish coastguard had dispatched the luxury cruise ship *Oceana Insignia* to rescue 68 migrants (and three corpses) that the crew of a merchant vessel had given aid to off the coast of the Tenerife. Two bodies were left in the Atlantic Ocean when the sea became too rough to retrieve them, but the cruise ship, which was on a 180-day round-the-world voyage with 670 passengers, brought the migrants safely to shore. It was a rare example of a cruise ship being used for migrant sea rescue in and around Europe, though it often happens in the Caribbean.

* * *

Staring at the coat and other debris floating in the water, Rita Catrambone and her husband Chris had a moment of awakening. They decided to invest their savings into creating a migrant rescue NGO, the Migrant Offshore Aid Station, or MOAS. It was the first private migrant rescue vessel to ever seek out migrant ships in distress, and it would become the model for more than 40 similar enterprises over the next ten years.

Chris Catrambone, the son of an American oil and gas engineer, was no stranger to strife and difficult situations. He made his millions with a war-zone specialist company called Tangiers International, which provides insurance coverage for kidnapping, terrorism and death and injury for private military contractors and freelance journalists working in some of the most dangerous places in the world. In 2022, Tangiers International acquired Malta's largest aviation insurance and risk management company, Osprey Insurance Brokers Co. Ltd, setting them apart from many other risk companies and putting them directly in the line of fire. MOAS seemed a perfect charity for the group, so they started setting it up when the 2013 summer season ended.

Prior to 2013, migrants in the Mediterranean were primarily rescued by Italian and Maltese coastguard and Navy vessels, and occasionally by merchant ships, which are generally unequipped to handle rescues. Few records were kept before 2013, but since then, the Missing Migrants Project has updated the toll, which in late 2024 totalled just over 30,000 people known to have been lost at sea over the preceding decade.

On 3 October 2013, everything changed. A migrant boat went down just a few miles from the island of Lampedusa, killing between 325 and 363 people, including many children. A week later, on 11 October, another migrant ship went down, this one carrying around two hundred migrants, that had allegedly been fired on by Libyan militias as it left Libyan waters, revealed in a report by Open Migration. The death toll has never been reliably ascertained. The twin disasters were a wake-up call for the then centre left-led Italian government, which responded by launching a national migrant rescue programme called Mare Nostrum ('Our Sea') in response to public outrage over the deaths.

The programme, which ran 323 dedicated naval vessels along with a submarine, helicopters and surveillance planes, and had a monthly budget of about $12m, actively searched for boats in distress and rescued 150,000 people. It ended on 31 October 2014, due to a shortage of both funding and political support, according to UNHCR briefing notes. The cessation of the expensive programme drew scorn from human rights groups, with the UNHCR warning, 'This will undoubtedly increase the risk for those trying to find safety in Europe, and could lead to more refugees and migrants perishing at sea.' When Mare Nostrum ended, MOAS had been operational for two weeks and was ready to step in.

The Catrambone family spent $8m of their own money on state-of-the art drones and kitting out a rescue ship called the *Phoenix*, complete with a field hospital, smaller rescue boats on winches, sleeping quarters for visiting journalists to bear witness, a full-time crew, and a canteen with a full-time cook. They hired professional sailing crews, rescue divers, and a small medical staff to aid migrants.

Usually, when migrants were rescued by Italian military assets, they were met with officers in hazmat suits and masks and forced to sit in rows on the cold ship deck. MOAS, and operations run by major NGOs like Médecins sans Frontières (Doctors without Borders) (MSF)) and Save the Children that followed it, greeted the migrants with handshakes and hugs. In a pre-COVID world, they found the idea of hazmat suits and masks unfriendly. The people they helped were called 'guests' and given back packs with donated fresh clothes and personal hygiene items. Interviews were conducted by social mediators who worked to understand what had led them to risk their lives. In 2020, British street artist Banksy entered the fray, funding a rescue boat, the *Louise Michel*, which has since been impounded and fined for its work aiding migrant boats in the Mediterranean Sea.

To some of MOAS's critics, philanthropist millionaires on fancy boats rescuing poor people sounded like a white saviour tax haven. Not only did Italian authorities scoff at what they described as a 'taxi service' to Italy, many right-wing governments across Europe expressed concern about private migrant rescue services becoming a 'pull factor' or enticement for smugglers, as described in a Cadmus policy brief. But despite the scepticism, MOAS was soon saving migrants at a time when countries in the region, like Italy and Greece, were facing fierce opposition to migrant rescue from the centre and extreme right-wing parties, which were gaining support. All of this at a time when the number of migrants was increasing, driven by the aftermath of the Arab Spring and other wars and conflicts. In 2013, more than 1.5 irregular million migrants and refugees sought shelter in Europe. The number had never been that high before (as stated by the Pew Research Center) and it hasn't been that high since. By contrast, in 1992, 700,000 people sought shelter in Europe after the fall of the Iron Curtain. Since that time, IOM figures show that irregular migration levels have fluctuated, with nearly 390,000 irregular migrants arriving in Europe in 2016, both by sea and by land through the Balkans.

MOAS became the model for all the subsequent rescue boats, including the NGOs SOS Méditerranée (France); Proactiva Open Arms (Spain); Sea-Watch, RESQSHIP Jugend Rettet and Mission Lifeline (Germany). These organisations also provided rooms for journalists to come on board and witness their work. The resulting coverage helped raise more funds, but inevitably, it drew negative attention too.

Since MOAS first set sail in 2014, more than 40 NGO rescue ships have launched into the central Mediterranean, according to the EU Agency for Fundamental Rights (FRA), almost all of which have been, at one time or another, under investigation, seized or blocked because they have been perceived as aiding and abetting irregular immigration. MOAS and several similar organisations eventually stopped sailing in the Mediterranean SAR area in 2017, after the right-wing Italian government signed a memorandum of understanding that could potentially force the rescue vessels to take those rescued at sea back to Libya, or to mandate that armed police would have to be on board all vessels. The added pressure of costly seizures and fines, which in 2023 rose to more than €10,000 per boat, also acted as a deterrent.

MOAS turned its efforts to rescuing Rohingya refugees in the Andaman Sea, and currently runs a field hospital in Ukraine, providing ambulances and paramedics to treat those injured in Russia's ongoing war. Several other boats, including those run by the charities Save the Children and MSF, also gave up rescue operations. MSF has since returned to sea rescue, pairing with various NGOs, but it has not had its own ship at sea since 2017.

In the summer of 2024, FRA reports, there were eight NGO rescue operations at sea and three small surveillance aeroplanes in operation. All eight faced sanctions and sequestering during the year.

* * *

The night before I boarded a French rescue ship in Catania, Sicily, during the summer of 2019, everyone got hammered. There was no alcohol allowed on board, so all the passengers, along with the Tasmanian captain and her Russian sailing crew, headed to a bar. It was an icebreaker of sorts, even if the contrast between our light-hearted mood and the life-and-death experiences we were about to witness was notable.

The charity rescue ships are a world of their own, long evolved from when the Catrambones dreamed up the idea on their yacht. The rescue crews are made up of a mix of humanitarians and regular sailors who might be on oil rigs or cargo ships at other times of the year. The Tasmanian captain of our ship was a long-time seawoman who had spent her career on various rescue missions, from icebreaking ships in the Arctic to the waters off the Gaza Strip. The sailing crew spoke exclusively in Russian and were rarely seen.

The sleeping quarters for journalists on the lower deck were understandably cramped. I was assigned a room with a French photojournalist who doubled as a belly dancer between assignments. We had spent the days before departure hanging around in Catania, waiting for various bureaucratic loopholes to close and for crew members to arrive. The operation's schedule was loose; no one knew exactly when the rescues would happen, which ports the Italian authorities would direct us to afterwards, or whether the boat would be sequestered. The crew had signed up for a three-month shift, and journalists had to commit to staying on board for a complete rescue. As we departed I was anxious, aware there was no way to know how long the ship would be at sea or where it would eventually dock.

We were on one of the original rescue ships run by the French NGO SOS Méditeranée. The onboard field hospital was operated by MSF, in what was at the time the first alliance of two NGOs working together on the same vessel. The onboard doctor was an Egyptian man on his first and, as it turned out, last rescue mission. The rescues would prove too psychologically difficult for him; so many of those we plucked out of the sea were his compatriots, often people whose upbringing was not so different from his own. Sometimes he couldn't hold back his tears as he worked.

As journalists, we were there to witness whatever happened, but we were also trained to help if needed. The law of the sea dictates that everyone on board a vessel must aid in a rescue. The

French belly dancer and I were in one room, and a German crew bunked next door. We surmised from mealtime conversations that they had far-right leanings and that their aim was to 'expose' the charities for complicity in illegal immigration. By the end of our mission, during which our ship rescued hundreds of people and we helplessly watched countless other humans sink to their deaths, one of the German journalists had decided to leave her field. She later started volunteering as a rescuer.

On the morning of departure, the mood was one of anticipation and mild hangover. The crew went over various safety procedures with all of us, and we practised CPR and evacuations and made sure the onboard morgue was ready. We set sail towards Libya in search of sinking migrant boats the way others might seek out sunken treasure, the crew scanning the horizon for any tiny lump that might be a target.

In its own way, rescuing is a business. By their own accounts, reported by Marketplace in 2023, it costs an NGO around $14,000 a day to run a ship. This includes the cost of the crew's salaries, fuel, medical supplies for rescued migrants, insurance, and other incidentals, not to mention food supplies, paying for unexpected maintenance on the ship, and the cost to dock at various ports. If the ship is out every single day of the year, the operating costs are more than $5m, roughly the same profit a migrant smuggler will get for the human cargo on one large boat the NGO will rescue.

Those who manage the ships range from humanitarian professionals to philanthropist hobbyists, and their economic motivations and rewards are varied. On one NGO ship I sailed with, the logistics chief was a NASA scientist from Florida who went out to sea once a year so he could get a tax break as a humanitarian. The main nurse on board, who doubled as a midwife, was retired and collected a comfortable salary from her work on the ship to supplement her pension. On the ships I sailed with, no one worked for free and the journalist observers were required to pay our way too.

After two days of sailing on the French craft, we were 'in luck'. The rescue crew heard about a boat in distress; we weren't told whether they picked this up on a radio frequency or from a more targeted call. I asked several times if the smugglers had contacted the crew directly, but the rescuers insisted that was not how it worked.

Migrant boats don't have sophisticated bridges with controls and radar. They are invariably stripped of everything but the engine and steering capabilities. There is no electricity, so mobile phones are generally dead after the first day, which makes sending coordinates very difficult. Sometimes smugglers give those who are in charge of navigation satellite phones, which do have coordinates, so when a migrant vessel makes a distress call to Maltese or Italian authorities, they might have coordinates. An NGO called Alarm Phone is often the first call migrant boats in distress make; many smugglers give the number to whoever is in charge of navigation. Alarm Phone then contacts Maltese, Italian or Greek authorities and generally posts updates on its social media about boats in distress. It also contacts NGO ships. However, since 2022 NGO migrant vessels can, under Italian law, be fined if they rescue migrants without being directed to by 'competent authorities', which means they have to wait to be told to rescue, or risk hefty fines and even being sequestered if they break the law.

But when I was on this particular ship, rescuers could still technically save whoever they found. Once the rescuers have the migrant boat in their sights, the larger vessel drops anchor and the action begins. People on the boats in distress react with what can only be described as panicked relief at the sight of another vessel, be it an NGO, an Italian coastguard or navy vessel, or even a merchant ship. Any ship represents hope, as long as it is not from the Libyan coastguard, who will push them back to Libya or even open fire.

The rescued people may not know the difference between an Italian military vessel or an NGO rescue mission, but they have usually been promised by smugglers that someone will 'meet' them at sea, so they assume whoever is approaching them has their best interests at heart.

The rescue operations are extremely dangerous for all involved, and the people on the migrant boats are at particular risk. Any movement or imbalance could sink them, and rescuers know that they have to approach slowly.

Life jackets are piled high on small rescuer speed boats that are launched towards the boat in distress. Arabic and French speakers accompany the smaller boat so they can shout out instructions in multiple languages. Rescuers dole out life jackets and take the babies and pregnant women off first. No one is rescued until all the babies have been handed over, and everyone else has a life jacket on. Large orange floats are kept on standby for anyone who falls into the water.

During the first rescue of the French mission, more than 200 people were brought safely to the larger rescue ship, ferried across in groups of ten. All the life jackets were removed and hosed down. Just as the people now safely on the ship were starting to settle down – changing out of wet clothes, drinking water, and using the portable toilets, the Tasmanian project leader said there was another boat in distress a few miles away. We were immediately on the move towards the next rescue.

As the next migrant boat came into sight, we suddenly saw a Libyan coastguard vessel speeding towards it. We were so close to Libya we could see land, and as we leaned over the top deck with our binoculars we were forced to helplessly watch a humanitarian disaster unfold. We saw panicked migrants jumping into the water as the notoriously merciless Libyan authorities violently pushed anyone they could reach onto their boat and headed back to Libya. No one was given life jackets. No one took the babies first. And no one came back to pick up the corpses left floating out at sea.

After the Libyan coastguard vessel departed to return the migrants on board to Libya, another boat approached the abandoned ship and set its engine on fire. There was still enough fuel in the engine to ensure that it went up in smoke within minutes, sending a thick black cloud into the air.

We made our way to where the burnt carcass of the boat smouldered. There was at least one burnt body in the water, but we couldn't retrieve it for the NGO ship's morgue. It was just too risky to get close to the still-burning boat because no one knew if there were gas canisters or flammable material on board. The NGO workers took photos to hand over to the authorities and we sailed away, all the while the migrants we had rescued watching in horror the scene they had narrowly escaped.

An hour later, the NGO rescuers heard of another boat that had just left Libya, and we headed in their direction. It was unlikely the Libyan coastguard would intercept two boats back to back. They don't want to intercept any at all, but they are obligated to do so under an agreement with the EU, especially in front of NGO ships that might have journalists aboard. They want everyone to know they are holding up their end of the deal they cut with Europe. Italian state vessels no longer take journalists on board, so there is no objective account of what happens if Libyans approach them during a rescue. These incidents are unreported.

The Libyan pushbacks delight the right-wing politicians in Europe who refer to migrants and refugees as 'illegals'. InfoMigrants reported in 2019 that Matteo Salvini, now Italy's deputy prime minister, insisted that Libya 'must be considered a reliable country where immigrants taken to the mainland by coastguards are safeguarded by the presence of IOM personnel. ' But the IOM doesn't condone the migrants being sent to Libya. 'IOM continues to advocate against the return of migrants to Libya as it cannot be considered a safe port,' it writes in its Libya fact sheet. Given the horrors that would-be migrants face in North Africa, this is something of an understatement.

Libyan detention centres are notoriously brutal, according to those who have been held in them, and according to authorities and groups like the Global Detention Project. 'Conditions at these facilities, many of which are under the control of militias, are deplorable,' the group writes in its description of the centres. 'There are frequent shortages of water and food; over-crowding is endemic; detainees can experience physical mistreatment and torture; forced labour and slavery are rife; and there is a stark absence of oversight.'

But, fixated on stemming the flow of migrants to its shores, Europe continues to make dubious deals with Libya. 'These arrangements include equipping Libyan forces to "rescue" intercepted migrants and refugees at sea, investing in detention centres, and paying militias to control migration.' Journalist Sally Hayden has documented the tangled relationship between European policy and the abuse, exploitation, trafficking and even murder of would-be refugees and migrants in North African detention centres in her book *My Fourth Time, We Drowned*.

* * *

Among the rescued people on this mission was a woman bleeding from her vagina; the midwife suspected a miscarriage. It was later revealed that she was haemorrhaging following a violent rape in the detention camps prior to her departure.

In 2023, I met a woman on a rescue vessel who had tried four times to cross the sea from Libya before finally making it onto an NGO rescue ship. Each time she was sent back to Libya, she was put in a detention centre, raped, beaten, and prostituted out to guards until she 'earned' enough money for another passage, which was arranged by someone inside the centre. Her hip had been displaced during a violent gang rape, and she walked with a limp. She told me that she had miscarried so many times she no longer menstruated. Her hands were covered with scabies scars and she was exhausted. But as we spoke on the rescue boat, she was happy to be alive. I still feared for her. Having escaped the hell of Libya, I felt sure that all that lay ahead for her was the hatred of Europe. Many migrants have no idea how much they are despised by those in Europe who see them as invaders, or how at risk they are of being exploited by those who see them as currency.

On the French vessel, the busy morning continued as the NGO rescuers prepared to meet the third boat in distress. This time it was a giant inflatable dinghy, loaded with so many people I couldn't even see the colour of the rubber. Hundreds of people straddled the sides, their bare feet dangling in the water. After hours or days at sea, people had been forced to relieve themselves in their clothing, and many were also covered in their own vomit from motion sickness. As the small NGO speed boat approached the dingy, babies were held high in the air. The rescuers began shouting instructions to stay calm, stay seated, don't stand.

Then, catastrophe. A commotion broke out, and all the passengers stood at once. The dinghy folded in the middle, sending at least a hundred people overboard. The rescuers hurled life jackets at people struggling in the water or clinging to the side of the dinghy. With horror, I registered that one of the babies had disappeared.

Two hours later, 242 people – all of those who had not drowned – were on the rescue vessel, along with those from the previous rescues. One man was in cardiac arrest and the main nurse performed CPR on him. The rescuers asked that he be airlifted to Sicily. It would be a few hours before the helicopter arrived.

A lightning storm started building under dark clouds in the distance, sending bright bolts into the water. I stood on deck, shocked by everything that had happened in just one day at sea. It was by far the most exhilarating experience of my professional life. It was incredible to think that the rescuers live through this regularly.

Once the last batch of rescued people were on the boat, the women and children were sent into a small section of the ship where they were was asked to take off their wet clothes in exchange for tracksuits donated by charity groups on the mainland. Many didn't want to give up their original clothing, having sewn gold chains into the seams, or written phone numbers on them. These were numbers they were supposed to call if they made it, and other numbers for someone else to call if they were found dead.

The rescuers allowed a few people to keep their clothes and everyone to keep their jewellery, but most of the clothes were put into large garbage bags to be thrown away on the mainland. The disposal of the clothing eventually got this NGO into trouble, when they were fined for illegal waste dumping after throwing the clothes into port dumpsters upon arrival. Inevitably, some knives, guns and small explosives were also found among the rescued people. Two women had held on to small handbags which were put in a secure place until the boat reached land. It was very hot on the boat and there were no showers for the rescued people who all had to use portable loos that were regularly disinfected. No one had shoes.

Everyone huddled in groups, but even in this stark survival scene, social hierarchies persisted. An Algerian woman with a bandage on her head said she had to have brain surgery in Paris in a month's time, but had been denied a visa so decided to travel this way. She was accompanied by a servant, who tried to make her comfortable, despite clearly being in shock after nearly dying at sea. At one point the Algerian woman asked if she could be in a private area, away from the darker-skinned people on the boat, whom she referred to as 'slaves', offering cash to the rescuers for better accommodation, which they refused. The medical team changed her bandages in the field hospital and sent her back, indignant, to sit with the rest of the rescued people. She was not the only one: other North Africans demanded to sleep away from the darker Africans, and some lighter-skinned men pushed darker ones into corners so they didn't have to be near them.

Six hours later, as most people were sleeping, the rescuers were alerted to another, larger boat in distress. The passengers stood watching from the various decks of the ship as another boat full of people was rescued, under strong spotlights that lit up the night sky. This time, it seemed, nobody fell into the water, or maybe the darkness just made them impossible to see. The NGO boat now had more than 600 migrants on board and had called Italian authorities requesting permission to dock at the nearest safe harbour. We had hoped to stop at Lampedusa, a couple of hours away. Instead, the ship was told to dock in Calabria, which meant a three-day journey.

After everyone had changed clothes, been fed, and settled down for the long route to Calabria, a young girl, maybe four years old, was found sitting alone. When asked her name, she said Mia, though she didn't know her last name. When asked where her parents were, she said they were with her and her baby sister. A frantic search of the entire boat led to the conclusion that her parents and young sister were not on board. Maybe they perished? I wondered whether her sister was the baby I saw disappear under the waves. Or perhaps she was just pushed onto the boat alone by people smugglers.

NGO rescuers tried to comfort her, but it was abundantly clear that this was not the first horror she had seen. Her eyes were vacant and she didn't cry even once. Over the course of the entire trip back to Italy, the rescuers, journalists and survivors took turns holding Mia and playing with her. She was fascinated by my blonde hair and kept wanting to comb it. Her hands were scarred from scabies, and her ribs were so sharp it hurt to hold her. She spoke Nigerian Pidgin English, which I could understand from interviewing Nigerian victims of sex trafficking.

Above: Mia with a rescuer.

At one point on the journey, the rescuers asked her and all the children to draw pictures. It's a form of therapy, but it also provides clues to what they have been through and where they are from. Mia drew her family, including a doll-like baby sister. Her father was very tall and thin, and wore a red shirt. Her mother had a scarf around her head and long braids. Mia didn't draw herself in the picture, but I didn't know how to ask why not. The rescuers surmised it was because she realised they were somewhere without her, and that she might never see them again.

When we got to the Italian mainland, she was one of the first people taken off the boat. She was handed over to Italian social services and put into foster care with other very young unaccompanied minors. I couldn't hold back the tears when they took her. I tried to check on her over the years, but after a period of time, privacy laws dictate that information can only be given to family members. A few years later, I got an email from one of the rescuers, who said Mia had been adopted by an Italian family and moved north to Milan, where she was going to a private school and doing well. I was so relieved; Mia could so have easily fallen into the hands of traffickers, groomed for sex or labour. She will never know what dream her parents likely gave their lives for. Perhaps her life is in some way what they would have hoped for.

After two days of sailing, the group was told they would disembark the next day in Italy. Celebrations broke out, and people began singing and dancing. The rescue team pulled out drums and other African musical instruments. Babies and children were placed on shoulders. The mood was light, with no premonition of the dangers that still lay ahead. I wondered if this was the happiest these people would be for a long time – maybe ever.

Inside each portable loo were signs in English, French and Arabic about how to spot the signs of trafficking, and giving the number of a French NGO to call if you believe you are a victim. This was terribly out of place on a rescue ship; something more appropriate for a public restroom in a shopping centre. I wondered how the boat's passengers were meant to access the information – almost no one had pens, paper or mobile phones, or if they did, the batteries were dead. When I called the number, no one ever answered.

A way forward

My time on the French rescue vessel left me with conflicting views of the work these NGOs do. There is no doubt that NGO ships save lives, conducting hundreds of rescues at sea. But some argue that they are an integral tool for the smugglers and traffickers, along with the European coastguard and other military rescue vessels. As a result, they have been accused of keeping traffickers in business, even if the assistance is not intentional or motivated by greed.

Frontex, Europe's tough border control unit, has pushed to invest in the coastguards of Libya and Tunisia. It has issued a number of reports, detailed by Eurac Research, purporting to prove that NGO rescue ships are 'pull factors'. NGOs have been targeted by criminal cases in both Italy and Germany. But Frontex also has assets at sea, and it has rescued migrants and brought them to safety without being accused of being a 'pull factor'.

It is not as simple as saying that rescuers' complicity drives trafficking. There is no data to suggest that more smuggler boats leave Tunisia and Libya when there are more rescue ships at sea, not least because there is no reliable data to prove when a smuggler ship leaves shore, and no way to know how long they are at sea before its passengers are rescued. There is no way to predict whether an NGO ship will make a rescue on its way to Libya, or when it will be routed to an Italian port. The variables are simply not stable enough, making evidence-based conclusions impossible to draw.

That said, it is known that smugglers send out boats whether or not rescue ships are patrolling. Smugglers and brokers advertise on Facebook and the dark web that the 'Red Cross,' which has never operated a rescue boat, and other groups including 'Italy' will rescue them at sea, but in reality NGO rescues are responsible for just a fraction of arrivals in Europe. Official data for 2023 published by the Italian coastguard shows that 8.5 per cent of the more than 157,000 people who arrived in Italy by sea were rescued by NGO boats. The rest were rescued by Italy's coastguard, Guardia di Finanza (financial police), and Navy assets, by Frontex or merchant ships; or they arrived at Lampedusa, Sicily and the Italian mainland on their own. In fact, more than 90 per cent of migrant boats that leave Libya and don't get pushed back by European border control, Frontex, or Libya's militant coastguard, are rescued by Italian military assets.

In October 2023, a prosecutor in Trapani, Sicily, issued a 650-page report (discussed in a Focus Online article) outlining how NGO boats may not be a pull factor, but in his opinion are a cog in the wheel of trafficking and smuggling. Among the damning evidence were first-hand accounts, mostly from journalists on board the ship *Juventa*, of what they saw, including members of the crew of a German-flagged vessel towing wooden migrant boats to Libyan coastguard officials, presumably for recycling by smugglers. The accused responded by commissioning a study from investigative research organisation Forensic Architecture presenting detailed evidence that police claims that the *Juventa* crew had been handing boats directly back to smugglers were incorrect.

The crew of the *Juventa* were exonerated in April 2024, but even left-leaning politicians have questioned the role NGOs play. A German parliamentarian told the Sicilian prosecutor:

> Many aid organisations make an important contribution to saving lives in the Mediterranean. However, a clear distinction must be made between saving lives and the calculated exploitation of civil commitment by criminal organisations. People smugglers exploit the hopes of

refugees by making false promises of a chance to stay and a better life in order to profit from the emergency. If it turns out that individual German sea rescue organisations have agreed to a systematic transfer hand-in-hand with smuggler networks, the constitutional state cannot simply look the other way. Because they are becoming complicit in an inhumane system. Such actions must be prosecuted. The perpetrators are increasing migration pressure and integration challenges, especially in Germany.

The rescue organisations in that specific case were later acquitted by a court based on lack of evidence.

This is the vexed backdrop which makes the humanitarian work of NGO rescue vessels so politically and morally complex. Perhaps if the NGOs operated in the countries of origin, or even transit countries such as Libya or Tunisia, they could help convince those with no chance of asylum not to risk their lives. But their biggest error may be their failure to have dedicated people on board rescue vessels looking for victims of trafficking, who might then be able to alert authorities on the ground about who is most vulnerable. As a journalist on several rescue missions, I was able to fairly easily surmise, by their age, who was likely being trafficked and who they were travelling with. A basic question like 'How much did you pay for passage?' could be revealing: if they told me someone else paid for them, or they had a job they were going to, it seemed clear to me they were likely being victimised. And yet all too often, it seems, there is nothing the rescuers can do to help. They seemingly have no liaisons on the ground in Italy with whom to raise a red flag, and there are no lists of vulnerable people beyond those who need obvious medical care, or unaccompanied minors like little Mia. Everyone else has to fend for themselves in a hostile environment. The traffickers are the only ones celebrating their arrival.

Follow the money

The more people are crammed onto the boat, the more it is worth to the smugglers who send it across the sea, and to the traffickers waiting for their human commodity to arrive. Consider a boat with around 400 migrants, who may or may not be trafficked, traveling from Libya or Tunisia to the Italian SAR zone. Each person would have paid – or a trafficker would have paid on their behalf – no less than $7,000, making the boat worth $2.8m or more. It seems to be general practice that young children and babies are often given discounts, though this is not always the case. It usually depends on their nationality; for example people from countries like Syria and Nigeria might be forced to pay for their children, while people from Ghana and Sudan, for example, may win the hearts of the smugglers and get a discount or free ride for no apparent reason at all other than the fact that many smugglers and brokers are from Ghana and Sudan.

Seven thousand dollars is a vast sum, especially considering that the cost of a one-way ticket on a state-run, safe, clean ferry from Tunisia to Palermo costs around $65, and comes with the option of a cabin for just a few dollars more. But a valid travel document is required to take an international ferry, and no one on the smuggler ships has been afforded any chance of obtaining the required visa, even though many would doubtless qualify if there was a way for them to seek asylum before risking their lives.

Falsified documents are commonly used, but they can cost thousands, even as much as a clandestine trip, and they don't always work, especially on the European side, where authorities are finding new ways to identify even the most convincing fake biometric documents.

Interviews with people I met on the French NGO rescue ship made it clear that almost every one of the more than 600 people rescued on the boat heading for Calabria had paid upwards of $7,000 for their trip, which would have netted the smugglers more than $4m. At the time of that particular rescue mission, there were twelve other rescue ships at sea. If each one rescued the same number of people in the same week, smugglers made more than $42m in a single seven-day period. And that is just for the smugglers.

Once the rescued people reach land, many of the women would have been forced into sex work to pay their traffickers around $30,000 through prostitution. Many of the men would have been made to work for a dollar an hour harvesting vegetables until they had paid at least $15,000 each to their 'owner' for the passage. Each person is worth around $50 a day for the state-sponsored migrant centres that house and feed them, most of which spend a fraction of that to care for them. The NGO ships cost a fortune to run, but they will also have raised funds for the rescue. A particularly eventful mission with drama and multiple rescues gets a lot of press and can help drive donations.

Prices for land travel vary greatly depending on the country of origin and how many international borders are crossed. To get to Europe from Pakistan, migrants pay around $6,000, according to the IOM. Global Initiative against Transnational Organized Crime suggests that, to enter from China, they pay at least three times more. Migrants and their traffickers pay between $2,000 and $10,000 to be smuggled into the US from Central and South America by land, according to the US Border Patrol.

Even the most casual watchers of European migration have a keen sense of the illegality tied to every facet of irregular migration to the continent. Money changing hands for unsafe passage is such a common occurrence it has become normalised. But from time to time, horrific tragedies and shipwrecks mark the rare instances when the world pays attention to what's happening, albeit briefly.

A sinking on 6 April 2011, which killed an estimated 150 people when a boat capsized near Lampedusa, made global headlines for the tragic loss of life. What no one talked about was the estimated value of $1m paid to smugglers for the doomed voyage. We don't know exactly how many people on that boat, or the 2013 wreck off Lampedusa that killed more than 350, were trafficked, but it's possible that for criminal gangs, their deaths could have represented losses in the millions.

CHAPTER 4

FASHION CRIMES

Sweatshops and forced labour

The flagship Prada boutique inside the Galleria Vittorio Emanuele II in Milan is a design Mecca. Its black and white tile floors and minty 'Prada green' decor are mirrored all over the world, from boutiques in Shanghai to the Prada Café in Harrod's, London. The nearly 1,600 square metre store, which today spans three levels, was opened in 1913 by Mario Prada. At the time, he sold English animal goods, including fur and leather, and imported steamer trunks to wealthy foreigners on European tours before later turning to Italian-made fashion.

The brand is under the watchful command of Mario Prada's granddaughter, Miuccia Prada. After taking on its leadership in the 1970s, she cemented its 'Made in Italy' focus. After a downward blip in the late 2000s, today the brand is comfortably back on top, cited as one of the most successful brands on the planet and worn by an A-list clientele that includes Margot Robbie, Taylor Swift, Rhianna, David Beckham and Justin Bieber. The house has also won a slew of awards and accolades across the world for its consistency as a representative of Italian design.

The price to keep the flagship property in its landmark spot is a cool €2.2m a year, but this is pocket change for a company that easily nets revenues of €4.2bn annually. It's nothing to pay upwards of $1,500 for a Prada bag or $3,500 for an off-the-rack dress. Miuccia Prada, now in her 70s, is still the brand's lead designer, and continues to be involved in the other brands that Prada has founded or acquired, which include Miu Miu, Church's, Car Shoe, Pasticceria Marchesi and Fondazione Prada.

I have visited Prada's finishing factories on various press junkets, and they are among the most luxurious in Italy. Promotional videos on the company's website show specialist craftspeople looking out on the rolling hills of Tuscany and forests in Le Marche as they put the finishing touches on all things Prada. Solar panels deliver renewable energy to the factories. Free parking and free childcare are just some of the perks Italian workers can enjoy if they sign up to working at Prada.

But the company has lately been grouped with some of the worst offenders in the apparel sector when it comes to having criminal forced labour in its supply chain. Human rights groups that monitor modern slavery have tried to pressure big fashion houses to pay closer attention to all aspects of supply chains, as reported by the Business and Human Rights Resource Centre. The group KnowTheChain rates fashion companies on an annual basis, evaluating policies, or what they say they do, and practices, or what they really do.

For example, in KnowTheChain's 2023 benchmark report on exploitation of labour in supply chains, the French company Kering, which owns Alexander McQueen and Gucci, scored just 23 out of 100 points. LVMH, which owns such brands as Christian Dior, Bulgari and Louis Vuitton, ranked even worse, scoring 6 out of 100 points in the 2024 report. Tapestry, which owns Coach and Kate Spade, scored just 16 points on the scale of

100. To its credit, Prada scored four points higher in 2023 than in 2021, but still reached only 9 points out of 100. Burberry scored 6, and Salvatore Ferragamo scored just 4.

The companies are measured using a methodology, based on the UN Guiding Principles on Business and Human Rights, which includes responding to accusations of exploitation, especially debt bondage, by workers in their supply chains. What this translates to is that if Prada commissions a company to produce a component like finely sewn lace, whether this is done in a factory in Bangladesh or central Italy, they need to do due diligence to make sure that the factory operates according to human rights standards. Failure to do this lowers the company's KnowTheChain ranking.

The *Wall Street Journal* found that in 2011 around 20 per cent of Prada's collections were found to be manufactured in China, and in 2023 Prada was among 40 brands identified by the European Trade Union Institute to be at high risk of sourcing clothing made from forced labourers in workshops known to be part of detainment camps for Muslim Uyghur prisoners. Uyghur detainees are also forced to pick cotton and weave cashmere, one of China's largest exports, according to a 2021 report by KnowTheChain. Prada did not respond to multiple requests for comment about their practices and KnowTheChain ranking, instead sending a link to its website:

> The supply chain of the Prada Group is completed with operators not related to the production cycle, among which are – as an example – the suppliers of commercial spaces, logistic services, media spaces, and services providers linked to the management of stores in the countries where the Group operates with

its retail activities; suppliers that, generally, are represented by large and primary companies. The Prada
Group believes that the risk of modern slavery within
its organisation is non-existent, while it deemed that
same risk as overall low along its external industrial
supply chain.

In the summer of 2024, Italian regulators, acting on a criminal
complaint against both the Armani Group and LVMH-owned Dior
Group, opened an investigation, reported by CNN, over claims
they make about their supply chains. Italy's anti-trust authority
said that the companies, which were being investigated separately
'may have issued untrue statements about their ethics and social
responsibility, in particular with regard to working conditions and
compliance with the law by their suppliers'. Both companies face
fines of up to €10m if they are found to be in violation of the law.

The probe comes on the heels of a criminal investigation
opened in March 2024 by Milan prosecutors against several
Chinese-owned firms in Italy which are part of the supply chains
for both Dior and Armani. The factories are accused of system-
atically abusing their employees.

Nasreen's story

Nasreen Sheikh doesn't really know how old she is. Born in a village
between Nepal and India, she doesn't have a birth certificate. She
was rescued by the NGO Walk Free from a T-shirt factory, where
she started working when she guesses she was around nine years
old. One of her earliest memories is being taken to a factory where
she and other girls her age, who she was told were her 'cousins',
were trained to sew. She was taken into a small room with no

window, where, along with five others, she was forced to sleep, live and work.

I met Nasreen years later, when she had become a spokesperson for Walk Free. She estimated that she was perhaps 30 years old at the time. Her hands were severely damaged and she was tiny, likely from malnourishment as a child. Her witness statement for Walk Free details her history.

> I worked 12 to 15 hours per day in a textile sweatshop, receiving less than the equivalent of US$2 per gruelling shift – but only if I completed the hundreds of garments demanded of me. I ate, slept, and toiled in a sweatshop workstation the size of a prison cell ... even then, I knew in my heart that people would not choose to purchase these items if they truly understood where they came from and how they were made.

She described how the days turned into nights, and said that her most important childhood memory was fear and the time she spent in the factory that made T-shirts for Western fashion brands. 'I had to stitch the same thing probably thousands and thousands of times. We also had a quota that I had to finish 600 or even 700 pieces sometime in a week,' she said.

She said many young women lost fingers and even hands in the sewing and cutting machines. 'If we lose our hand in that process, or if we lose our eyes or have some accident or injury happens, we will never be able to make a police report because we don't have any documents,' she said, adding that if they didn't finish all the garments by the deadline, they wouldn't be paid for any of the work. 'I would just cry.'

The factory closed down shortly after she started, and she was pushed onto the streets and eventually into a forced marriage. 'I was exposed to the street, and that is how in Nepal so many women and girls get pulled into sex trafficking,' she said.

Luckily, she was taken in by a man who eventually allowed her to go to school and tried to find her family. She learned that her entire family had been trafficked. Her father worked in a car factory, eventually succumbing to brain damage from the fumes he was exposed to. Her uncle lost his sight working in a welding factory. Her sister was forced into marriage at the age of 12 and had her first of six children by the time she was 15. 'They get forced into that situation to become a baby-making machine that eventually serves the corporation's needs,' she said. 'They go overseas and work with unregulated manufacturers, and these unregulated manufacturers use undocumented people like us who are very voiceless.'

Nasreen became an advocate.

After breaking free from my exploitation, I came to America and went to a large chain store for the first time. I walked the aisles in disbelief looking at the thousands of products available to purchase in one location. I had never experienced this level of both luxury and convenience, but it was horrifying to connect with the reality of how these products had likely come to be. When I gazed upon the countless consumer goods as I walked from aisle to aisle, I couldn't help but see the faces of children in each of them, of men's and women's lives marred by poverty, inhumane working conditions and unimaginable exploitation. The suffering woven into each fibre and reflecting on every surface. That night I just wept in pain for this world.

* * *

It's not just in Asia that garment workers are exploited. Even in the heart of Italy, sweatshops have become all too common, and not just for disposable fast fashion retailers. Big brands also commission components from factories with questionable practices.

The city of Prato near Florence is where some of the fashion world's most important designer creations get their finishing touches, the quintessential core of the Made in Italy brand. But when you drive into the city, the first thing you notice is the Chinese language signage.

The Chinese presence in Prato is now long established. On a reporting trip there in 2007 to interview Paolo Zegna of the Ermenegildo Zegna fashion house about the emergence of Chinese sweatshops, I was astonished. Italy is one of the most monocultural places in the world: overwhelmingly white and Christian, according to the most recent census data. It is also one of the hardest places to integrate; in 2020 it scored just 58 points out of 100 on the Migrant Integration Policy Index, which measures things like how a country allows foreigners access to its culture, how welcome they feel, and access to naturalisation. So, in terms of its ostensible multiculturalism, with Chinese restaurants, shops and language in evidence, Prato is an extreme outlier.

Zenga was there in his capacity as president of the Federation of Italian Textiles and Fashion Enterprises. He told me then that Italians were outsourcing too much of their handiwork, which would eventually damage the reputation of the country's long-standing brand image. At the time, some big brands were changing their labelling from 'Made in Italy' to, for example, 'Made by Benetton'. Others decided to keep production in Italy, at any cost – even if it meant the products wouldn't be made by Italians. It was around that time that a slew of new factories opened in the Tuscan town, made possible by incentives geared towards Chinese investors.

I returned again in 2013 to report on a related tragedy. Bad wiring had caused an electrical circuit to short in one of the newer Chinese-owned factories, which turned out to be a cover for a sweatshop. Seven undocumented workers were killed in the late-night fire. The factory was producing components for fast fashion and big designer brands alike and specialised in pieces that needed to be glued, which meant there were chemicals on site. An investigation revealed a lack of inspections and checks. The fire revealed first-hand the seedy underworld of high fashion, and how rapidly Prato had turned into a Chinese enclave.

The victims' charred bodies showed signs of abuse and none was ever positively identified, nor were their bodies repatriated. They were not only undocumented workers, like so many forced into labour in Europe, but they had no officially traceable identity. Those whose fingerprints could still be taken were unmatchable to any database accessible to Italian authorities. It was almost as if they never existed at all. Even calls to China to try to identify who they were turned up nothing.

What was soon apparent was that these dead workers were the tip of an iceberg, and that the fashion factories that dot Italy had become a breeding ground for the type of forced labour more often identified in countries like Bangladesh, Vietnam and India.

After the tragic fire, the factory was closed down and a sting operation of similar structures in the area, as reported by

The Diplomat and InfoMigrants, found that many of the Tuscan factories were violating basic human rights norms, ranging from housing undocumented workers in illegally built dormitories on site, to not providing proper safety gear to people working with hazardous materials. Hundreds of workers were rescued from surrounding factories, revealing the extent to which the European fashion industry had become reliant on systematic labour trafficking. The rescued people were given an opportunity to go back to China. Some who chose to stay were given asylum, and started factories and other businesses of their own.

The official 2023 Italian census lists around 31,482 Chinese immigrants in Prato, but the actual number is likely closer to 75,000, according to local police estimates. Officially, there are 5,000 textile factories with 40,000 registered workers. That leaves at least 30,000 workers unaccounted for. GRETA has expressed concern that while anti-trafficking measures do exist on paper, the implementation of such protections is lacking because of the tendency to group together all irregular migrants, whether they are refugees, seasonal labourers or other migrants. 'GRETA is concerned that the restrictive immigration measures adopted by Italy foster a climate of criminalisation of migrants, resulting in many potential victims of trafficking not reporting their cases for fear of detention and deportation,' its 2024 report states.

Workers reported to police I talked with that they had been forced to sleep in hollowed-out cardboard boxes stacked to look like factory inventory, so that if police raided the premises they would not draw suspicion. Many of the workers who have either been rescued or arrested said they worked for 14 hours a day or more and were never allowed to leave the factory, even for a walk or to get fresh air. Meals were brought in. Because they had no legal documents, they were made to believe they couldn't even walk down the street without being arrested and thrown in jail.

* * *

There are two tiers of Chinese-owned factories in Prato: the underground sweatshops that run in windowless warehouses; and the more upmarket factories that operate legally. Both are part of fast fashion and luxury fashion supply chains. In many cases, the sweatshops provide items to the legitimate factories, which then provide items used in both fast fashion, like Zara and Mango, and high fashion products like Dior and Armani, according to GRETA's 2024 investigation, including handsewn items that end up in Gucci, Prada and other Italian fashion brands. But in some cases, the sweatshops also supply items directly to fashion houses, according to the Milan investigators looking into the Armani and Dior groups.

Luxury goods constitute more than 5 per cent of Italy's GDP, with fashion accounting for half of that, making it one of the most important industries in the country. Fast fashion in Italy, increasingly called the 'beauty economy', which includes cheap knock-off designs and beauty products and accessories that are primarily sold online, has grown to account for 26 per cent of Italy's GDP, according to a 2023 survey by Banca Ifis. The exponential growth of these industries has produced jobs that are not appealing to Italians, which has in turn driven trafficking, according to Dr Jerónimo Montero, a researcher with the University of Manchester. 'The conditions are horrendous. But if that isn't enough, one labour inspector told me that with the little money they earned, the workers had to pay off the costs of being trafficked into Italy,' he said. 'It takes up to four years to pay off the debt, and only then are they free to leave these awful places.'

Chinese investments in Europe started to grow after 2016, thanks to changes in the exchange rate and a softening of previously prohibitive regulations and taxes on foreign investments. Then, in 2019, Italy became the only G7 nation to sign up to China's trade and investment Belt and Road project under the government of the anti-establishment Five Star movement. Opportunities for Chinese investment in the country exploded. Italy eventually withdrew from the Belt and Road in 2023 under the government of Giorgia Meloni, which had vehemently opposed it in the first place, but by then Chinese companies had established a strong presence in the country. According to Reuters, Meloni denied widespread reports that she was pressured to withdraw by the US Biden administration under President Joe Biden.

Many Chinese-state owned companies in Europe are now under investigation for labour rights violations, and a handful have been sanctioned or even closed after it emerged that they were employing Chinese citizens who had been illegally trafficked into Europe. In April 2024, the China Chamber of Commerce to the European Union condemned the crackdown, especially in the sector of Chinese wind turbine suppliers, calling the results unfair. 'This action sends a detrimental signal to the world, suggesting discrimination against Chinese enterprises and endorsing protectionism,' it wrote in an open letter.

* * *

Forced labour is not only a problem in the north of Italy. Five years after the factory fire in Prato, another anti-trafficking sting operation was carried out in the southern Italian region of Campania, where much of the detailed leatherwork is done for high-end French companies. Authorities found workshops full of pregnant trafficked Nigerian women working unthinkable hours. The anti-trafficking group Be Free, which rescued many of the victims, found that they had been transferred from performing forced sex work until they gave birth. Some had miscarried on the factory floor and had been forced to continue working, being careful not to get blood on the leather, survivors told police. Others who miscarried were sent straight back to the streets to replace other women who had fallen pregnant.

The experiences of trafficked workers in Italy are horrific, but for many working for Italian brands outside its borders, things are even worse and have been for decades. In her 2007 book *Deluxe: How Luxury Lost Its Luster* investigative journalist Dana Thomas wrote about an interview she had with an investigator who visited a factory in Thailand tied to some of Italy's best-known fashion names. The investigator told her:

> I remember walking into an assembly plant in Thailand a couple of years ago and seeing six or seven little children, all under 10 years old, sitting on the floor assembling counterfeit leather handbags. The owners had broken the children's legs and tied the lower leg to the thigh so the bones wouldn't mend. [They] did it because the children said they wanted to go outside and play.

A *New York Times* investigation in 2018 uncovered another way big brands get around accountability issues when it comes to supply chain labour. In southern regions of Italy, impoverished Italians and immigrants alike are hired to do detail work from home for factories that produce apparel for brands like Max Mara, Fendi, Armani and Louis Vuitton. The workers, mostly women, would be paid around $1.50 an hour for sewing on sequins or attaching lace to collars and lapels at their dining room tables. Others are paid by the yard to hand-sew coats that will eventually bear the Max Mara label. A seamstress would make around $25 to hand-sew a coat that retails for more than $2,000. One woman interviewed told the *New York Times* she tried to sew two coats a day, working nearly 15 hours to earn a meagre living of $50 a day. If she damaged the material, her pay was docked. While the US's federal minimum wage is $7.25, and the UK's is £11.44, the fact that Italy does not have a federally mandated minimum wage made the abuse legal.

When you consider that Italian citizens living in their own homes with full rights under Italy's strict labour laws are still working under such dismal conditions, it speaks volumes about how unseen workers are treated. The Italian woman who made $50 a day made four times as much as a trafficked woman who did the same job inside the factories. As the factories they make the coats for did not bear the brand names that eventually ended up on the garments, the brands could avoid exposure. Instead, the coats were sold in bulk to another company, which then sold them on to Max Mara, the *New York Times* report found. The only thing left to do in the Max Mara-branded factories was to sew on the monogrammed buttons and labels.

Supply chain issues are not limited to Made in Italy brands. In 2022, Walk Free issued a study on modern slavery in the fashion industry which found that G20 countries annually import around $148bn worth of apparel goods and $13bn worth of textiles that are at risk of being produced by forced labour. They point out that risks of modern slavery exist 'at each stage of the garment supply chain, from growing and producing raw materials, to processing these into inputs, to manufacturing'. Children are especially vulnerable to forced labour in developing nations, based on demographics of known trafficking victims reported by organisations that save them, and while often these children are not necessarily trafficked between countries, they are often sold between factories and treated like slaves.

It seems incredible that prestigious brands could be employing child slave labourers, but fashion companies often turn a blind eye to the activities in the factories that produce smaller component items within their supply chains and instead try to focus consumers' attention on the end-of-the-line factories that assemble the final product, which tend to be held to a higher standard. Big name brands like Prada, Gucci and Dior earn consumers' trust with marketing images that show craftsmen at work in artisanal surroundings, as if to imply the entire supply chain is in one place. More than likely, according to Remake, the factories these images show only put the finishing touches on the products, a standard practice among all the top designers.

* * *

The role of Chinese trafficking in the Italian fashion industry is just one way that Asian criminal networks intersect with the European economy. Prosecutors in a 2017 investigation, as reported by Reuters, alleged that rampant money laundering had led to more than $4.5bn in cash being smuggled out of Italy to China by Chinese citizens working in the garment district in Prato and Florence. The state-run Bank of China was ordered to pay Italy some $22m in back taxes tied to the money laundering scheme, but Italian investigators were unsure where the money had been made, whether in the fashion factories themselves, or funnelled through them from other illicit businesses. It was also unclear who was directly involved and how they physically smuggled the cash, in euros, back to China. Did they travel on falsified documents or did they have work permits? Once in China, did they hand the money to authorities, since it was tied to China's state bank? The questions have never been answered, but police have also uncovered Chinese mafia-style groups operating drugs and prostitution rings out of Prato, trafficking women for the sex industry and young men to ferry drugs from storage areas to local clients. In some cases, the mules ferried cloth and other fashion accessories smuggled in from China without duty being paid. The fraud went beyond Chinese-owned businesses and extended to other factories, part of a larger scam in the area.

The 2017 investigation by Italy's Guardia di Finanza (GDF) led to an even bigger revelation: the Bank of China was running a complex underground financial system that was laundering up to €2bn a year by sending money to prominent Chinese state banks through legitimate cloud-based internet wire services. Clients included South American drug traffickers and Russian oligarchs who have since lost their right to make traceable purchases in Italy, thanks to sanctions tied to Russia's invasion of Ukraine. There were also wealthy Chinese citizens involved, who wanted access to luxury Italian fashions, according to the court dossier.

The scam, which was uncovered by the GDF, also revealed that Italy's Mafia-tied groups were using underground banks to launder money and hide cross-border payments. An officer with the GDF (who preferred to remain anonymous) told me in an interview that the system is not so different from the hawala system favoured in the Middle East. She explained that as Italy's often archaic banking sector modernises, it has skipped several steps, going straight from in-person banking to cloud-based systems that make it much easier to hide money. She estimated that more than half the money laundered by the Chinese banks came from forced labour trafficking.

In the autumn of 2023, Europol reported that 58 people arrested in Italy and 20 in Spain were tied to illegal Chinese money brokers who were accused of drug trafficking and trafficking irregular migrants to work as drug mules. Investigators said the criminal group turned a profit of $44.2m on 30 million tonnes of hashish and marijuana sold illegally across Europe, according to Reuters. The criminal group had been using the Chinese money traders to launder the drug trafficking profits, much like US money traders handle Latin American drug cartel profits. On the periphery of the ring were forced sex workers and drug mules who had all been trafficked from China into Italy.

Moving people clandestinely from China to Europe is an expensive endeavour that can top $30,000 per person. The traffickers, who generally have ties to the garment industry or the drug trade, provide the labour, while the workers' salaries, if you can call them that, go directly to pay off their trafficker. Even those who were forced to sleep in horrific conditions on-site at the garment factory were forced to pay for room and board, as dismal as it was. They are never given a choice, and, in fact, they are told if they left the premises, the Italian police would throw them in prison, according to the few who have been rescued.

The number of Chinese asylum seekers has spiked in recent years, increasing by a magnitude of five over the last decade. *The Guardian* reports that many who leave cite an escalating atmosphere of state repression as a push factor. Those who are smuggled out of China are vulnerable to being trafficked, first to neighbouring countries and then into Europe and the US, according to Europol. The incidence of Chinese women trafficked into forced prostitution has grown substantially in recent decades, according to INTAP Europe. In 2020, seven people were arrested in Colombia after recruiting Chinese women via social media. The women agreed to move to Colombia because they were told they would become pseudo wives for wealthy Colombian men. In reality, the women were trafficked for work in fetish brothels.

Trafficking into China is also a problem. In 2019, authorities in China found 45 North Korean women who had been sold to underground Chinese brothels after escaping the oppressive dictatorship of Kim Jong Un. They were subject to everything from systematic rape to forced pregnancy to produce offspring, as reported by *Forbes*. The Committee for Human Rights in North Korea revealed that in a few of the cases, so-called aid groups that had helped the North Korean women escape were actually covers for traffickers who ran a $105m-a-year business selling North Korean women to Chinese traffickers. Some of the women were sold on and ended up in Europe. Among them were several North Korean victims who had been sold into sex work when they were just nine years old.

A way forward

The rate of forced labour used to make high-end luxury goods is three to four times higher in Italy than in other countries that produce luxury good in large quantities, such as Bangladesh, India, Vietnam and Myanmar, according to Lieutenant Colonel Loris Baldassarre, who is leading the investigation in Milan into the Dior and Gucci groups. 'In developing nations people are exploited and paid slave wages,' he said. 'But here in Italy, people are trafficked in to do the work, hidden away in factories and treated like animals.' One of the reasons that Italy ranks so much higher than places like Vietnam, which is notorious for low wages and underpaying local staff, is because in Italy the exploited workers are mostly trafficked, and have no legal means to file a grievance or even complain without risk of deportation, as the 2023 GRETA report found.

Walking through the streets of Prato, it seems impossible that in a tight-knit garment town like this, locals don't know what's going on in the factory next door,. Don't they notice that no employees are ever seen entering or leaving the building? Some of the factories don't even have employee parking areas. And how can it be that workers in the finishing factories can open a box of finely hand-crafted components to be assembled into expensive garments and not be aware that the person who made them is 'paying back' his or her trafficker instead of receiving a salary? As long as it's not happening in the factory that sews on the designer label and hands the final goods to the designer company, things continue at pace. The discrepancy between how little accountability these factories face and the meticulous image that is presented of brands' finishing factories is mind-numbing.

Unfortunately, a culture of silence hangs over the industry. What authorities discovered after the Chinese workers died in that fatal 2013 fire was that most of the trafficked workers in European factories were too afraid to even talk about their treatment. Survivors who were rescued from the burnt Prato factory refused to cooperate or testify against the factory owners out of fear they would be punished.

Fast fashion brands and luxury brands alike turn a blind eye to human rights abuses. Less than 5 per cent of fashion companies at either end of the price spectrum scored 'good' or 'great' on the group Good On You's 2023 survey of fashion crimes. Big brands talk the talk, but often hide a compromised supply chain behind 'for show' finishing factories. And some 33 per cent of modern slavery statements by large luxury brands do not even meet minimum requirements, according to the KnowTheChain survey. More than a quarter of the companies in the most recent report don't disclose information about their supply chains, even though there is no doubt they know exactly where every single component comes from – and how much it costs.

Labour trafficking in all manufacturing industries, including fashion supply chain factories, relies on the same techniques. Falsifying records is one of the main scams that factories that use trafficked workers rely on. Falsifying records allows companies to conceal tax withholding as well as excessive overtime, according to the ILO. 'Companies may create a second set of fabricated records, known as "double book-keeping", to convince auditors they have been correctly paying workers their wages, retirement contributions, and other benefits when they have not,' according to the 2023 Trafficking in Persons report by the US State Department. 'In other cases, manufacturers may alter pay slips to conceal prohibited wage deductions or overtime work.'

Employers who rely on trafficked workers to turn a profit also consistently falsify workers' identities, including their age, citizenship and immigration status. In some cases, they even falsify dental and medical records to conceal trafficking victims. The US State Department report also found instances where factories that used trafficked labour doctored up a second set of identity documents for underage or exploited workers 'in case' they were audited. These employers frequently retained the identity documents and passports of exploited workers, in part to stop them from going to law enforcement for help. Some of the worst violations concerned Bangladeshi workers in the Maldives, Bhutanese students in work–study programs in Japan and Malaysia, and Zimbabwean domestic workers in Oman, according to the ILO. 'Human rights groups have documented instances where migrant workers' access to their passports is manipulated to deceive auditors, such as when passports were stored in guarded lockers, but the workers were only given keys and able to access their documents during audits,' the State Department found.

Victims are also coached to lie about conditions, including their pay, the hours they work, and the conditions they work in. 'Human Rights Watch found evidence of factory managers intimidating workers into lying, sometimes telling workers that a negative audit could cost them their jobs,' the report says. A common ploy is that supervisors and complicit colleagues are always around when exploited workers are interviewed by auditors, which prohibits them from being honest about their situation. Brainwashing is a common tool used by traffickers to keep victims complicit. In many cases, the victims are isolated in the country they have entered and only know their traffickers. 'In other instances, the manipulation of workers extends beyond coaching. In some cases, manufacturers have instructed underage workers to hide from auditors, either off-site or in hidden areas of the factory during the audit,' Human Rights Watch says.

Fighting this facet of forced labour has proved extremely difficult because so much money runs through these factories. 'Manufacturers have an incentive to deceive auditors precisely because audits increasingly affect brands' decisions on which suppliers they will and will not use,' the US State Department warns. In response to the problem, Human Rights Watch and other groups have devised a list of recommendations, including conducting unannounced audits and interviewing suspected victims of trafficking off-site.

Journalist Dana Thomas sums up the underlying dynamics that perpetuate this scourge: 'The global fashion supply chain is in essence a corporate form of colonialism, and the underpaid and badly treated workers are just one step up from slaves. Indeed, there is slavery in the supply chain, and prison labour. The mind reels.'

Follow the money

The luxury market is as complicit in the scourge of human trafficking as the fast fashion market, fighting to produce inventory with the greatest profit margin. Like every single sector of trafficking, forced labour in the fashion industry would not exist if consumers made smarter choices. Detecting human trafficking may be complex, but it is relatively simple to establish when a purchase is unethical in a more general sense.

We've all seen advertisements for cheap clothes on social media and online shops and in discount stores. The $10 dress that keeps popping up on your feed may be cute, but it has a hefty price tag in terms of the human suffering it cost to produce. Arguably, no reputable fashion company that follows the norms and practices of basic human rights can produce a $10 dress in bulk without cutting corners. Dressember is a human trafficking advocacy company run by Blythe Hill, who decided back in 2005 that she would give up her cheap fashion and spend more on clothes by wearing a dress every day and encouraging others to do the same.

She did not buy $10 dresses; she spent money to support companies that had clean supply chains after she learned the horrific truth that more than four million people worldwide make less than $2 an hour to feed the need for cheap clothes, according to the ILO. Many of these people work in developing nations, and most are women with no access to healthcare or other benefits.

In 2013, when the Rana Plaza sweatshop collapsed in Dhaka, Bangladesh, more than 1,100 garment workers were killed while they were making clothes for 29 major brands like Zara, Primark, Walmart, JCPenney, Mango, Matalan and Benetton, according to investigators who used the labels on the clothing in the rubble as evidence. More than 2,500 workers sustained injuries, some resulting in amputations. Since that time, almost nothing has changed in terms of companies relying on cheap factories who employ modern-day slaves to produce cheap clothes for the West. Blythe Hill says:

> When we dig deeper into the production of the things we buy, we can avoid supporting companies that are perpetuating fast fashion, human trafficking and environmental degradation. Ethical fashion brands are often extremely open with their methods of production. Our everyday choices are making a difference in the world, even when it doesn't feel that way. When we choose to hold off on buying a $10 dress from one store and decide to save up for a fairly made $60 dress, we are sending the fashion industry a powerful message.

The average garment worker in Bangladesh makes $95.50 a month, according to the ILO. That's up from $68 a month, which was the going rate at the time the Rana Plaza collapsed. Children as young as 12 years old are 'legally' employed in Cambodia and Bangladesh, where the largest fast fashion factories run 24 hours a day, according to Human Rights Watch. That means they don't go to school and will never escape the cycle of poverty. Human Rights Watch's report 'Paying for a Bus Ticket and Expecting to Fly' blames both consumers of cheap clothes and those who market and produce them. 'Low purchase prices and shorter times for manufacturing products, coupled with poor forecasting, unfair penalties, and poor payment terms, exacerbate risks for labour abuses in factories,' the report authors contend. They also believe that the market demand makes it impossible for producers not to ignore their bottom line, meaning they have to produce more and more inventory to sell at lower and lower prices:

> Often, bad purchasing practices directly undermine efforts brands are making to try to ensure rights-respecting conditions in the factories that produce their wares. They squeeze suppliers so hard financially that the suppliers face powerful incentives to cut costs in ways that exacerbate workplace abuses and heighten brands' exposure to human rights risks. Many brands demand their suppliers maintain rights-respecting workplaces, but then incentivise them to do the opposite.

There is some hope amid the despair. Recently, H&M and Adidas made public disclosures about who their manufacturers are, which transferred pressure down the line and put some of the weight on the shoulders of the factories, which in their anonymity often get a pass. This opens the door for groups working to identify factories that utilise trafficked people, so that those larger fashion houses can be made aware. Ultimately, more ethical manufacturing is within our reach if we push for it: Human Rights Watch estimates that it would take just a 12-cent increase in the price of a basic T-shirt at H&M or Walmart to provide a living wage for workers in developing nations. The issue remains in the hands of the consumer. If we stop buying cheap fashion, we stop funding trafficking in this sector. And if fashion labels are going to incentivise factories to do better and follow more ethical practices, we consumers must commit to pay more for that.

CHAPTER 5

MISSING IN ACTION

Surrogacy and adoption in love and war

For years, refugees from warring African nations have been system-
atically blocked at European borders. After 24 February 2022,
these same borders suddenly opened to Ukrainians fleeing the
Russian invasion. The European Think Tanks Group, an umbrella
group of European associations and foundations working towards
global sustainability, quickly pointed out the stark hypocrisy. 'The
EU's robust and unified response is to be welcomed. However, it is
hard to ignore how much the narratives of solidarity and expansive
policies towards Ukrainian refugees contrast to the increasingly
restrictive policies and hardening rhetoric more commonly seen
as a response to other refugees arriving in Europe,' they wrote in
December 2022, ten months into the ongoing war. 'There can be
little doubt we are witnessing the emergence of a racialised refugee
hierarchy in several EU member states.'

Behind the shocking outbreak of war in Europe lay another
controversy about the movement of people across borders. In
recent years, Ukraine had also become one of the world's premier
countries for surrogacy, described as 'one of the most important
destinations for fertility travel worldwide,' in the journal *Medical
Anthropology*.

The war in Ukraine sparked fierce, overdue debate in fertility circles about surrogate mothers' rights to make decisions about the foetus she is carrying based on her safety. When missiles started flying over Ukraine, many commissioning parents, known in the industry as intended parents, or IPs, started insisting their surrogates leave Ukraine even when the pregnant women did not want to be separated from their families, especially those with husbands suddenly drawn into combat.

The COVID-19 pandemic had brought similar challenges, with hundreds of babies born to surrogates at a time when travel bans made it difficult for their IPs to collect them. Ukrainian surrogacy agencies like BioTexCom, one of the largest in Ukraine, posted videos on YouTube showing rows of uncollected wailing infants during lockdown, and urging leaders to open borders. The video garnered mixed reactions and gave those against surrogacy plenty of ammunition to criticise the fertility industry. But ultimately, pandemic travel, while restricted, did allow for family reunification, enabling many IPs to collect their children. What is hard to trace is just what happens to babies who are not picked up.

Tabatha and Wayne's story

In 2020, Tabatha and Wayne (not their real names), a young professional American couple living in Los Angeles, found out they couldn't conceive naturally, putting their dream of building a family in doubt. They began the arduous journey of assisted fertility, investing thousands of dollars in IVF over the course of 18 months, only to be disappointed each time. After several unsuccessful tries, their fertility specialist suggested surrogacy with donor eggs, which they explored locally.

In an interview with me over Zoom, Tabatha and Wayne said they couldn't find any agency that would charge less than $170,000 for agency fees, insurance, legal costs and the expensive healthcare required by assisted fertility and childbirth in America. Because Tabatha's eggs were not viable, they also had to pay for donor eggs, although this is in fact cheaper than the hormonal treatments required to extract Tabatha's eggs would have been. All included, they were looking at nearly $200,000 for one try. And with the average rate of success less than 50 per cent, even for the youngest, healthiest egg donor and surrogate, the costs could have quickly climbed.

At a cocktail party, Tabatha and Wayne ran into another American couple who had had the same problem, but were now gushing over the impending birth of their second child. The mother-to-be, who was clearly not pregnant herself, explained that they had found the solution in Ukraine

They had learned that Ukraine was one of the world's largest surrogacy-for-hire economies in the world. But unlike other previous high-turnout countries like India and Thailand, where the health and rights of surrogates were often in doubt, Ukrainian surrogacy seemed relatively safe and ethical. In 2015, both Thailand and India banned commercial surrogacy to foreign nationals after a number of horrific stories emerged about how the surrogates were treated and how some foreign couples who commissioned surrogates took only one twin or changed their minds.

Commercial or altruistic surrogacy for foreigners is still banned in India, though altruistic surrogacy is available to Indian nationals. But in Thailand, according to the Voice of America, efforts were well under way in 2024 to reverse the ban and open up commercial surrogacy to the international market. The proposed legislation to lift the ban, according to the *Bangkok Post*, also includes the option for intended parents to bring surrogates to the country to gestate.

There is no question that surrogacy is a political hot potato. Pope Francis has condemned it and Italian Prime Minister Giorgia Meloni has worked to criminalise it. Ukraine, which is vying for EU membership, will face some pushback on its liberal surrogacy enterprise. In January 2024, the European Council sought to add illegal adoption and surrogacy as types of exploitation covered by the European Union's anti-trafficking law. The EU eventually adopted a watered-down version of the proposed amendment to add just the words 'exploitation of surrogate motherhood', aimed at 'persons who force women to act as surrogate mothers or who trick them into doing so' to anti-human trafficking legislation, which leaves interpretation up to each member state, as reported by the European Institute of Bioethics.

Before Russia's invasion of Ukraine, surrogacy agencies provided bespoke services based on individual family request, including choosing the diet for surrogate mothers and laying out other restrictions, including whether she could have sexual intercourse while pregnant, and the types of tests and supplements she would be required to take. The surrogates were often from Russia or Georgia and had similar profiles – they were educated, healthy, and treated surrogacy professionally.

For Tabatha and Wayne, reviews on fertility discussion sites on Reddit and Facebook left by happy couples who realised their dreams in Ukraine were more than convincing. Many had had more than one child through Ukrainian surrogates, which was made easier as most agencies also provided embryo storage options, meaning that those wanting larger families could use the same egg donor more than once.

At the time Tabatha and Wayne decided to use the Ukraine-based agency, about 2,500 babies were being born every year to surrogates in Ukraine, according to *The Economist*. These babies were successfully transferred to their paying biological parents, or IPs, at birth as long as one of the parents could prove they were genetically tied to the new-born through a DNA test – all provided by the clinics – to facilitate the paperwork within the rather loose constraints of the Ukrainian government.

According to some of the surrogacy companies themselves, 80 per cent of Ukraine's surrogate children were born to foreign couples. After a small decline in surrogacy contracts tied to the COVID-19 pandemic, business had grown. The whole surrogacy package, on average, started at just over $30,000, with the surrogate mother receiving a third or more of the total fee. The price scale reflected the amount of waiting time and the number of tries the infertile couple would like to have with the same surrogate. The highest-priced packages included unlimited tries and had a waiting time of less than six months. In 2023 these cost just over $70,000 – still far less than the most basic surrogacy service in the US.

Tabatha and Wayne immediately arranged a trip to visit Kyiv's largest clinic. There they found similar American couples on the same journey to parenthood, and ended up forging friendships. They chose a mid-range package, which included DNA testing for Wayne after the birth to prove a genetic relationship and obtaining a passport for the baby under their name. A donor egg was chosen from a woman with a biological profile and appearance as close to Tabatha's as possible, and the insemination produced seven viable embryos. The couple decided to implant three, which produced twins, at no extra charge. The surrogate agreed to carry them to term. Tabatha and Wayne were thrilled.

Their babies were due in April 2022. They booked their return trip and accommodations in Kyiv far ahead of the birth, in case the surrogate delivered early, and busily prepared the nursery back in Los Angeles.

On 24 February 2022, Tabatha and Wayne woke to the news of Russia's invasion of Ukraine. They hoped it would be a short-lived attack, but as the days wore on, it proved to be anything but. Their surrogate was in her final trimester and living on the outskirts of Kyiv, where some of the worst fighting was playing out. Horrified, Tabatha and Wayne watched the war unfold on live television news. The Ukrainian telecommunications system had been badly damaged and they couldn't reach the surrogacy agency by phone or email. The silence was deafening. Tabatha watched the endless barrage of Russian missiles and feared that even if their surrogate had found shelter, the trauma could affect the pregnancy.

When they finally reached the surrogacy agency more than a week after the invasion began, they were told that their surrogate had been moved to the Hotel Venice in Kyiv, along with all the surrogate mothers in the programme who were in their final trimester. More than fifty women were seeking shelter in the hotel, often hobbling down to the basement bomb shelter, terrified and in tears, doing their best to stay calm as their pregnancies wore on.

Three months later, when the twins were due, the war had reached fever pitch. No country was allowing any of its citizens to travel to Ukraine, even by train from Poland. Tabatha and Wayne had explored the possibility of moving their surrogate to Poland to give birth there, but it was enormously costly and complex. The surrogate had her own children and needed to move them to Poland with her. The agency couldn't even give an estimate of how much it would cost; in the middle of the war, they would have had to hire an armoured car and a private security service, arrange for accommodation and childcare for the surrogate's children, and since the surrogate wasn't an EU citizen, she couldn't access state-run European health programmes, so they would also have to pay for private hospital care.

Legally, the plan was also problematic. Since surrogacy is illegal in Poland, once born, the children would have belonged to the surrogate until Tabatha and Wayne could effectively adopt them, or take them back to Ukraine to do the paperwork.

In the end, Tabatha and Wayne made the excruciating decision not to move their surrogate, leaving their unborn twins to an uncertain fate. They felt they had no choice but to terminate the surrogacy contract, based on the fact that they could not get to Ukraine to pick up the children. The idea that their babies could end up victims of war weighed heavily on them. But so did the debt they were quickly accruing. They decided to adopt a child in the US and have started to build a family that way.

Tabatha and Wayne's twins were part of a group of almost 50 active pregnancies after Russia's invasion abandoned by the parents who commissioned the surrogates. The babies' fates remain a cause for concern.

When I asked Tabatha about the possibility that the babies had been aborted in the third trimester, she said she hoped that they would have been given up for adoption instead.

Tabatha and Wayne tried to find out what happened to their twins after the birth date, but since in the agency's view they had reneged on their contract, they were told they had no rights to further information. Tabatha says she tried to reach out to the surrogate many times, but was never successful. By the time travel restrictions started to loosen and people could travel into Ukraine at their own risk, the twins would have been nearly a year old, if they had been carried to term.

A year after the war started, Ukrainian surrogacy was back in operation with many of the surrogates gestating outside the country, crossing the border to deliver in Ukraine, and then leaving again. The costs have risen slightly to reflect that change.

Interpol has stated that the fate of those surrogate babies is likely representative of all the Ukrainian surrogate pregnancies in course when the war started. Of 40 of the babies who were born from the 50 original foetuses, ten were kept to be raised by the surrogates, who had no biological connection to the babies at all; a further ten were eventually claimed by the families who commissioned them after the surrogates met them in third countries, including one who was more than a year old and who had been living in foster care. The remaining 20 babies were taken by Russian military forces as part of a widespread 'evacuation' of Ukrainian children to Russia, who numbered around 19,000 as of the summer of 2024, according to a France 24 report. These children were given Russian citizenship in a decree signed by Russian president Vladimir Putin in January 2024, an attempt to 'keep the children out of harm's way'. Ukraine's foreign ministry accused Russia of using the stolen children to solve its 'demographic crisis'. But many of these children have been forced into military service or given to Russian families to either raise or force to work. Russia admits to taking the children and claims they were removed for 'their own safety'. The families of the missing children have pleaded with international authorities to intervene, with little success.

It is one of the most blatant examples of child trafficking in modern times, but child exploitation under the shadow of war is not new. The removal of the children by Russia from Ukraine was carried out with the world watching. Nearly 400 children have been returned to Ukraine, either through rescue operations or mediations carried out mostly by Qatar. But the rest of those children will likely remain in Russia for the foreseeable future. For those who are very young, that could be long enough for them to forget their Ukrainian identity. For all of them, it is long enough to fall into exploitation.

War and child trafficking go hand in hand. More than 105,000 children have been exploited as child soldiers between 2005 and 2002, according to UNICEF. These children are categorised as 'child soldiers', but the aid group says only a few end up in combat. The girls are often sexually exploited and boys who don't fight are often used as messengers, cooks and guards. 'While living among armed actors, children experience unconscionable forms of violence,' UNICEF warns. 'They may be required to participate in harrowing training or initiation ceremonies, to undergo hazardous labour or to engage in combat with great risk of death, chronic injury and disability.' They might also be malnourished, forced to take drugs to be compliant, and often face even greater problems when and if they are returned to their families.

* * *

BioTexCom, Kyiv's largest surrogacy agency, had been in the spotlight long before the COVID-19 pandemic and the outbreak of war. In 2011, its founder, Albert Tochilovsky, was criminally investigated for human trafficking after a Spanish couple learned that the baby their surrogate carried through the agency was not biologically related to them. Their embryos, it appeared, had been 'inadvertently' mixed up along the way, the agency said, and the Spanish couple were essentially 'sold' a baby other than their own. The fate of their embryos remains the subject of a civil legal action against the agency.

Tochilovsky eventually beat the criminal charges after convincing prosecutors that it was the maternity hospital, not his agency, that mixed up the babies, but he was investigated again in 2016 and 2019 after surrogates complained their wombs had been removed during birth, which they say was arranged by the clinic. His clinic is also part of an Interpol investigation into the sale of foetuses for medical research, which would constitute trafficking of embryos without consent of the parents.

When I reached out for comment, BioTexCom wrote in an email that all charges against them had been dropped, and that because the Interpol investigation remained ongoing, they could not comment, on the advice of their lawyer. Several requests to interview Tochilovsky were refused.

* * *

In the UK and Canada, paying for surrogacy is illegal, but in the US and Ukraine it remains big business. Global Market Insights calculate that the global business of surrogacy turned over around $14bn in 2022, and is expected to hit $129bn by 2032.

Long before the modern phenomenon of surrogacy, there were records of 'baby farms', places where women had babies for the purpose of selling them for profit, dating back to the 19th century in the UK and the US. Both countries banned the practice in the

1920s, according to the Adoption History Project run by the University of Oregon. But baby farms remain a concern in some places. In 2021, the Dutch government put a stop to all adoptions from abroad after a highly critical report (as outlined by the BBC in that year) found that many children being adopted out of Sri Lanka in former decades were either stolen children or babies born in baby farms, where women had been held captive, impregnated and forced to have children to be sold through the illegal adoption scheme (as described by *Dutch News*). The practice was discovered when a woman who was adopted by a Dutch family in 1992 tried to trace her biological history. She learned that her birth certificate was forged and that her biological mother was impossible to find. She sued the Dutch government in 2022 for not scrutinising the practice, and is awaiting a final decision in early 2025.

More than 170,000 babies were adopted from South Korean 'orphanages' during the 1980s and 1990s, in a practice that is just coming to light in recent years as those adopted out realise that they may have been 'given up' for adoption without their parents' knowledge, or sold on, sometimes under different identities. In August 2023, Arrows of God Community Children's Home in Anambra State, Nigeria, was closed after an undercover journalist from the Foundation for Investigative Journalism revealed that the orphanage was willing to sell him a baby for a little under the equivalent of £1,000 (reported by the Nigerian *Guardian*). The owner of the facility was apprehended in June 2024, according to *The Punch*.

In 2018, two decades after her death, the BBC reported that Mother Teresa's Missionaries of Charity was investigated for child trafficking after one of the nuns who worked in Kolkata sold a 14-day-old baby for around $1,500 to a couple who later reported it to police. Indian officials inspected all the holy sisters' homes, closing down at least one over allegations of child trafficking, according to Reuters. And while there is no proof Mother Teresa herself had any knowledge of trafficking that may have happened when she was alive, it is indisputable that her charities took part in the sale of babies to adoptive couples, and that the Vatican Bank ultimately took those profits. Her charity bank account remains active, despite the accusations, undoubtedly because of the amount held in it. 'They have said that at least five to six babies have been sold to childless couples,' Aman Kumar, a police officer, told the Thomson Reuters Foundation. 'We are investigating to see how the operation was run and how many more children have been given away in the last few years.' The charity claimed that police were treating Mother Teresa's organisation like a 'criminal gang' but admitted the practice of taking money for adoption should not have been allowed.

A way forward

The sale of babies by a Catholic charity calls to mind my own great-grandmother's alleged adoption. I can only try to imagine the circumstances under which she was given up or taken away, and how much money the Austrian couple might have paid for her. Disturbing as it is, there is no way to find out the truth. Contemporary Afghan records of birth certificates and adoptions are out of reach, if they exist at all. And, with its devastating history of war and political instability, I wonder how many children are being trafficked there today. The US State Department classifies Afghanistan as a Tier 3 country with no known protocols to protect children against exploitation, either through illegal adoptions or recruiting children as child soldiers.

In July 2024, a US court nullified the adoption of an Afghan child by a US service member a year before the chaotic days of America's withdrawal from the country. The infant, thought to be six to eight weeks old, was found abandoned on a battlefield after a US strike. Marine attorney Joshua Mast, who was in the country at the time, petitioned a military court for emergency adoption, which was granted to him and his wife back in the US. The baby's immediate family had been killed in the strike, but Mast's desire to adopt the baby was disputed by the child's uncle, who petitioned the Taliban-led government to intervene. The Virginia court ruled that Mast misrepresented the facts in his assertion that there were no living relatives. Thus, the adoption was cancelled and the baby repatriated to join her surviving family members. The judge wrote that because there was no country agency involved in the adoption, it had to be voided.

Stories like Mast's highlight how complex the ethics of international adoption and surrogacy can be. The majority of international adoption and surrogacy programmes are legitimate. But when they go wrong, either through deliberate wrongdoing or due to geopolitical upheaval, they highlight how vulnerable babies and children are to being trafficked. Infertile couples are often willing to go to extremes to build families. Traffickers and unscrupulous adoption agencies feed on that desperation, which is part of what keeps the illicit business of selling babies alive, according to UNHCR.

UNHCR has very clear guidelines prohibiting the sale of children, based on the 1993 Hague Convention on the protection of children. But in inter-country adoptions, these guidelines are not always enforced. Often, families are told they are saving children from otherwise horrific situations, without knowing that, in many cases, the agencies involved created those situations, sometimes by forcing the biological mother to have the baby in the first place, or by preying on people in extreme poverty and pressuring them to sell their children, which the UNHCR defines in a 2022 press release as 'enabling environments' for illegal adoptions.

One strategy to address the issue is ensuring that international protocols match, meaning a family from the UK, where adoption rules are very strict, should have to follow these rules even if adopting a child from a country like Uganda or India, where there are fewer checks. The UN also calls for prohibiting private or independent adoptions, which are those that operate outside the official structures and often take place family-to-family rather than through official agencies, where substantial payments can be made.

Universal background checks to ensure the 'adoptability' of any child in an orphanage and protocols which ensure the biological parents are informed, are often ignored in high-value transactions between agencies and future parents. In the US, the Adoption Network Law Center has been the subject of intense scrutiny after several former employees exposed the murky business of paid adoptions for a *Time* magazine exposé in 2021. Among the allegations, including a criminal complaint that the company settled in 2006 by paying $100,000 in fines, the company is accused of coercing pregnant women who enquired about adoption to move to states where adoption laws are lenient to start the process. The birth mothers were then required to sign a legal agreement that mirrored surrogacy agreements, complete with handsome payments and veiled threats that if they backed out of the contract and decided to keep their babies, they would be liable for all costs. Because private adoption in the US is legal in many states and largely unregulated beyond the stipulation that babies must be born on American soil, it has become a lucrative enterprise, with brokers matching adoptive parents to birth mothers for a handsome fee. Often these adoption and surrogacy companies feel more like a 'do-it-yourself' endeavour, with those suffering from infertility going online to find impoverished birth mothers who feel they have no choice but to give up their babies.

Children trafficked for illegal adoption are frequently from developing nations, or areas where war or massive natural disasters have caused widespread displacement. Babies may literally be pulled out of camps for displaced people, away from parents who might be injured or separated or, in the case of the American Marine, picked up off the battlefield. There are few uniform protections for these vulnerable children, especially to and from countries that are not signatories of the 1993 Hague Convention.

On a basic level, the UN calls for the abolition of humanitarian aid that is linked to authorisation of adoptions, and for charitable donations to be separated from any adoption process.

Follow the money

In the 1920s, the going rate for buying a baby in the US was around $100 (equivalent to about $1,398, or £1,094, today), which could be paid for in instalments after an initial down payment, according to the Adoption History Project. Advertisements went so far as to promise: 'It's cheaper and easier to buy a baby for $100.00 than to have one of your own.'

Modern illegal adoption is not as costly as one might think. Hartini Zainudin, a children's welfare activist who works in Malaysia, says the cost of a baby on the Malaysian illegal adoption market ranges from $400 to $7,500, with the more expensive babies being those with lighter skin. Zainudin's charity has 'bought' scores of babies from would-be illegal adoption agencies in sting operations that rescued the children and closed down the baby shops.

The director of the Malaysian NGO Tenaganita, Aegile Fernandez, says that migrant women and teenagers from wealthy families who do not want the stigma of a child out of wedlock are often those whose babies end up on the black market, netting middlemen and traffickers thousands of dollars. 'Women were being brought in for the purpose of a job, but they were then kept locked up, confined, then subsequently raped and then the babies were being sold,' she said in an interview with me. 'These babies are bought by syndicates. These children, when they come to the age of eight, are then used for sex work for paedophiles.'

At the other end of the legal and ethical scale, being a legitimate paid surrogate can be a very lucrative business, according to those who have done it. A surrogate in Ukraine who did not want to be named because she was still employed, told me that she receives around $250 for an embryo transfer, whether or not it results in a viable pregnancy. If she donates her own eggs for her or another surrogate, that will earn her an additional $600 per egg. Paid egg donors in the US earn around $10,000 in comparison, but are more closely vetted, according to several surrogacy agencies interviewed for this book.

Surrogacy agreements vary, the most lucrative being those with the most restrictions set by the IPs who contract the births, but will generally net the surrogate $15,000 in Ukraine and as much as $60,000 in the US. Surrogates with previous experience often make bonuses in both countries.

CHAPTER 6

THE DARKEST SIDE OF TRAFFICKING

Child sexual exploitation

The first time I came face to face with trafficking was when I set foot in a muddy refugee camp on the border between Kosovo and Albania in the spring of 1999. I was pregnant, and the smell of sewage under the hot sun was nauseating. Brown and white tents were lined up close to each other. Privacy was non-existent. Women hung the laundry washed in communal tubs over the entrances of their tents. Flies were thick in the air.

There were conspicuously few men, young or old. Most had been killed or died in battle in what was, at the time, the most headline-grabbing war in the world. I wasn't the only pregnant woman there, of course. There were thousands of ethnic Albanian Kosovar women forced from their homes during the war who were also pregnant, most as a result of brutal rape, which had become a widespread weapon of torture, especially when carried out in front of the victim's children or husband.

The dynamics of the camp hierarchy were clear. The pregnant women were largely safe, despite the questionable circumstances under which they had conceived. But during the aftermath of the war, which started in February 1998 and ended in June 1999, with NATO airstrikes, younger women and teenage girls started disappearing one by one, plucked out of the chaos to be sold into the forced sex industry across Europe, largely run at that time by Russian mafia and Albanian criminal gangs.

Things were desperate in the region and no one in the refugee camp wanted to go back to whatever was left of their bombed-out homes, which made the young women perfect victims for traffickers. Deprived of hope, they were promised residency in France, Italy or Spain. They were given falsified documents to gain entry to the EU – a classic staple of debt bondage – which paved the way for them to become sex slaves in lucrative human trafficking schemes. The women's and girls' virginities, which were increasingly rare due to the rapes, were auctioned off, and deflowerings were filmed as a right of passage before they were forced to sell their bodies as fully fledged prostitutes.

In the 25 years since I saw young women disappearing from the refugee camps the Kosovo war produced, sex trafficking has exploded to become the most lucrative form of trafficking. Records of the number of victims of sex trafficking are hard to come by before the world started taking notice around 2000 with the UNODC protocol, but since then, the number of known victims has quadrupled worldwide, according to both Eurostat and UNODC. Many of the Kosovan victims were under 18, a reflection of the darkest side of the trafficking trade, where sex trafficking meets child exploitation.

Daisy's story

'Daisy', as she was called in the Italian criminal dossier investigating her suspected murder, was one of the thousands (as reported by CNN in 2024) of unaccompanied minors who have disappeared in recent years after arriving in Europe via Italy on the irregular migration trail. Research by the organisation Lost in Europe, a cross-border journalism project investigating the disappearance of child migrants in Europe, found that at least 51,433 unaccompanied refugee minors were registered as missing between 2021 and the end of 2023 in 31 European countries, including Italy and Germany.

Daisy's documented story began when she was rescued by an NGO charity vessel at sea in late 2019. She then spent some time in Catania, Sicily, at a religious centre that housed unaccompanied minors. Her time there was during Italy's harsh COVID pandemic lockdowns. She was only 12, but she looked older in both the mugshot taken when she entered Italy, and in the horrific photos that eventually surfaced on the web.

No one knows exactly when she fell through the cracks. She was likely kidnapped when out on a walk, investigators speculated. They believe that she was almost certainly from Ethiopia, based on her facial features, though the records at the centre where she was last seen listed her as Nigerian.

At the time, school classes were being held online in Italy, and movement of any kind, including irregular migration into the country, had all but stopped, making it especially difficult for traffickers to find victims. Asylum application processing had also stopped. Desperate for new human commodities, traffickers disguised as delivery people began lurking around migrant centres, officials from Italy's anti-trafficking unit explained when I interviewed them. Asylum application processing had also stopped during the pandemic, since most of Italy's bureaucratic offices were closed and the country's government infrastructure had not been digitised, meaning people couldn't work from home, even if they had computers or bandwidth available with their children doing online classes. People were stuck and movement was stalled, but trafficking continued.

The officials stated that hundreds of young adolescent girls disappeared from centres for unaccompanied minors during that time. Most were written off as runaways, even though strict patrolling by Italian authorities to stop the spread of COVID-19 meant that anyone who left their residence had to carry a piece of paper explaining why they should be allowed to legally leave their homes. But no one checked delivery trucks and couriers. One of them could have taken Daisy from the asylum centre.

Efforts to trace Daisy's whereabouts turned up nothing. She did not appear at her asylum hearing in 2021, and no one knew where she had gone. The centre where she was staying, which has since been closed due to maltreatment of children, marked her down as a runaway. An investigator who looked into the centre's alleged crimes hypothesised that she may even have been sold by staff. Centres in Italy get a government stipend for each migrant they house. Filing a missing person report reduces their income.

Daisy was next seen in a series of pornographic films on the dark web, where she was often tied up and gagged. Her last appearance was on a snuff film channel which subscribers to the live feed paid more than $500 to watch.

Some of the most disturbing media imaginable, snuff films are productions in which the subjects are killed, or appear to be killed, often during sexual abuse. They are disturbingly more common than one might imagine, but they are not new. Even before the internet and streaming and the dark web, snuff films were ordered and delivered in the regular post, often in plain envelopes or disguised as other types of films.

Neapolitan police, working with British agents, analysed the final film, in which Daisy was abused by a masked man and a woman whose face is off screen. Their research determined that the film was almost certainly shot in Russia. And they believe that in it, Daisy was killed.

* * *

Father Fortunato di Noto is a Sicilian prelate who founded the group Meter, named after the Greek word for mother. He is a pioneer in exposing the prevalence of online paedopornography. I first met him in the late 1990s when he feared, presciently, that the nascent internet would become a hotbed of illicit activity. He successfully petitioned the Italian parliament to set up the Italian Convention, a landmark ruling that went beyond the 1989 New York Convention on the rights of children to extend to protection online. At the time, he was already working to save children from victims of paedo-criminality, as he called it. In the years since, he has seen unthinkable images.

His research turns up results that are beyond horrifying and he has faced severe backlash and allegations that he and the priests and nuns who were rooting around in the depths of the internet in search of child pornography were somehow self-serving, as he recalled in an interview with me in 2019. Others have questioned his role in investigating sex crimes when the Catholic Church has been mired in persistent sexual abuse scandals. In a 2019 interview, Father di Noto responded to questions about the behaviour of some of his colleague priests and the persistent cover-ups, victimisation and abuse of minors in the Church, saying 'Abuse is abuse, no matter where it comes from', adding, 'We must listen to the victims ... We will not win, but we have to fight. We will not save all the children, but for some we have to do it.'

He and those who work with his group comb the internet and dark web looking for child victims. When they find websites and evidence of abuse, they frequently take photos or print them out, since many sites are only up for a short time: ISPs and web servers are changed frequently to keep these sites hidden. Meter's specially trained team members check the web 24 hours a day. There are also psychologists on hand to help the researchers cope with what they find, and staff work hand-in-hand with Italian police.

Meter has reported to police 30 million photos and videos of sexually abused children ranging in age from a few days to 13 years old, on 134,222 websites both on the traditional internet and the dark web. Among them are thousands of images of newborn babies. Di Noto's work has led to 23 international operations and his group has saved 1,600 victims worldwide, mostly unaccompanied migrant children and foster care charges who were being exploited in the most unthinkable ways.

Thanks to di Noto's work, in 2010, scores of Germans, Italians and Americans were arrested by Interpol, the FBI and local law enforcement authorities in those nations and put under investigation for either purchasing or seeking to purchase snuff films involving children that were shot and produced in Russia. The films had been sent in the post, but the Neapolitan investigators intercepted hundreds of them in Italy and delivered them to intended recipients in street clothes. Once the consignee signed for the package, officers pounced and arrested them. The parcels went to 600 different homes. The 500 people who were eventually arrested had paid between $60 and $120 per film, depending on the degree of violence. Three Russians were also identified, but never arrested due to jurisdictional complications.

As the BBC was reporting over twenty years ago, Russia has a history as a major centre for the production of child porn. In 2000, a 30-year-old Russian car mechanic named Dmitry Vladimirovich Kuznetsov was arrested in the UK after sending more than 3,000 bespoke videos of children who appeared to die during physical and sexual abuse to paying clients in Italy. The case was handled by prosecutors in Naples, one of whom explained to me that some clients had ordered films dealing with specific fetish abuse, ranging from forcing underage children to have sex to bestiality. A few of the film buyers were investigated, but no one apart from Kuznetsov was ever arrested.

According to investigators, unaccompanied migrant minors are often the victims of choice for the makers of child pornography. And as the story of Daisy shows, children are not only abducted in war zones or as they make hazardous journeys. Overwhelmed immigration systems and poor safeguarding mean that kids are easily smuggled out of migrant centres and foster homes, and because immigration systems are often overwhelmed and understaffed, they are almost never searched for.

A 14-year-old Ukrainian girl named 'Daria', profiled in a US State Department report on child trafficking tied to Russia's invasion of Ukraine, lost her parents in a Russian airstrike and was shuttled to the UK, where a family member helped her apply for asylum. While living in a shelter for refugee children during the lengthy asylum process, she was approached by a trafficker who promised her a better place to stay than the dismal shelter, as well as a waitressing job to help her earn some spending money. With coaching from the trafficker, she was able to convince the shelter that she was staying with a relative. At first, she later told British investigators, she was pleased that the man gave her English lessons and a bedroom in his own home, even though the waitressing job never materialised,

Within a few weeks, the man was plying Daria with drugs and sexually abusing her, and within a month prostituting her out to a clientele that included pornographers. He told her that if she reported him, her asylum application would be nullified. Police eventually rescued her in a sting operation involving other young war refugees, including a number of adolescent boys, who had been tricked into leaving state-run shelters and who all ended up being trafficked for sex. The shelter where she was originally being housed continued to take the government stipend for her care long after she left, and it was only during a routine audit that authorities even realised she had never checked back in with officials after she left. Daria turned 15 in a new shelter and was granted asylum, but has since returned to Ukraine.

It's not just girls who are at risk. In UNODC's 2022 Global Report on Trafficking in Persons, boys under the age of 18 represent the fastest-growing segment of people identified as trafficking victims. The number of boys and young men identified as being trafficked for sex quintupled between 2004 and 2020. After that, figures are skewed by the pandemic lockdowns, but the trend was on the rise and can be expected to continue. The reason behind this growth is that young male prostitutes command higher fees on the street that their female counterparts, even though the majority of clients of prostitution are males looking for females.

Regardless of their gender, unaccompanied minors on the migration trails are extremely vulnerable. Sometimes they travel with siblings and get separated, other times their parents die along the journey, and sometimes they are being trafficked by adults who have helpers shepherd them through the labyrinth.

On an NGO rescue ship in 2016, I watched as an older Nigerian woman coached a group of about a dozen young Nigerian girls, not one of them older than 15, to lie about their age – to say they were 24 – and giving them stern looks when rescuers asked too many questions. As she coached them in Pidgin English, the French and Italian boat staff looked on, oblivious.

I approached many of the girls to interview them, but the older woman – a madam of some sort – brushed me away, saying the girls were tired, under stress or needed to rest. I spoke to some of the girls around the boat when they went to fill their water bottles or use the toilet. One young girl told me the older woman was her aunt, and that all the girls were cousins. Based on their appearance, I knew that was not likely. I questioned her about what she would do once she arrived in Europe. The aunt was taking them to a nursery school where they would all work as babysitters, she told me happily.

As a journalist, I was only meant to act as an observer on the boat. But I knew they were being trafficked, and felt I had to intervene. When I alerted the staff, they said there was nothing they could really do. Their job was rescue and delivery; that was enough. Seeing a dozen girls falling through the cracks in front of so many people who could have saved them haunts me to this day. None of us did what we could or should have. We watched them slip away.

* * *

The British toddler Madeleine McCann disappeared from a family resort in the Algarve in 2007. As of September 2022, the Metropolitan Police disclosed that it had spent nearly £13m on

Operation Grange, the code name for the investigation into her disappearance. The figure only includes expenditure for British officers, not for the many Portuguese and now German officers who have worked on the case.

Missing migrant children are not the same as other missing children. By comparison, no money has been allocated specifically to search for unaccompanied minor migrant children who disappear in Europe, of whom there had been 18,000 between 2018 and 2020, when the last data was published. Money is spent on migrants and refugees who disappear only if they are involved in criminal investigations.

Today the search for McCann continues across Europe. Investigations in Germany suggest she may have ended up the victim of a child trafficking ring, according to German investigators I spoke with in 2022. At the time of writing, the only formal suspect in her disappearance and presumed murder was Christian Brückner, a German convicted of sexual offences who was working as a handyman in the resort where the McCanns were staying when Madeleine disappeared. He is currently serving a seven-year sentence for the rape of a 72-year-old woman. Investigators have tried to unravel the suspected sex trafficking ring they say he was involved with. Searches of the camper van he used at the time turned up little girls' swimsuits and CDs full of often violent pornography involving children. Investigators are still working to identify as many of the young victims as they can to see if any were reported as missing children and to try to determine just who these young girls who appeared in the films are. In October 2024, Brückner was acquitted of five rape charges in Portugal, and will be released when he finishes his seven-year sentence.

McCann's case in the context of global sex trafficking is important because it demonstrates differing attitudes towards children believed to have fallen into the hands of traffickers. In McCann's case, millions of pounds have been spent to find her, with hundreds of officers dedicated to follow various threads that have ultimately led them to the German suspect. While McCann's case is horrific when looked at through any lens, so are the cases of the hundreds of thousands of missing unaccompanied minors. The only difference is where the children happen to come from.

Paedo-pornography is a multi-billion dollar business that serves a growing number of fetishists, as reported by Global Initiative against Transnational Organized Crime. And the industry thrives on the fact that the disappearances of migrant children are not tracked. The fact that they don't have identity papers makes them easier to victimise, an officer with Interpol once explained to me. 'They are ghosts. They are literally invisible victims that no one can save because no one knows who they are.' And they are not the only ones to suffer the consequences. As the investigator pointed out, 'The dark web provides inspiration for the worst of humanity. Everything is possible there.'

Anyone can find themselves a victim of the violence that some consumers of this content go on to commit. In 2017 Danish scientist Peter Madsen lured the award-winning Swedish journalist Kim Wall, whose work appeared regularly in the *New York Times* and *Harper's*, into his homemade submarine, where he raped, murdered and dismembered her. A catalogue of women being beheaded, tortured and impaled on metal spikes was found by investigators on his hard drive, along with explicit content depicting children. Madsen was ultimately convicted of premeditated murder based on his internet searches and catalogue of horrific snuff films. But it is hard not to be disappointed that little was done to find out who those victims on those hours of film that inspired him were. His conviction was deemed a success, but when I asked investigators in Copenhagen about what they were doing to pursue justice for the victims in the films, they said that the films were not made in Denmark, so it was out of their jurisdiction.

The videos exist and are in the hands of law enforcement, but the victims' identities remain unknown, and their bodies have never been found. This lack of action remains one of the biggest black holes in helping victims of this vulgar form of trafficking.

A way forward

A group of a dozen middle-aged German men looking for a kinky weekend pull up at a hotel on the Via Domitiana in Castel Volturno, southern Italy, where they have pre-arranged the services of 24 Nigerian women who are all in slavery with the same Nigerian madam. She has charged the men a fair price, she feels, and the girls will share a room separate from the sex rooms to shower and change costumes, but all 24 will be available from Friday to Sunday, 24 hours a day, with no breaks. The women have no choice but to take the job, and for many of them, it is a welcome relief from giving blow jobs to the truck drivers and anal sex to the priests who form their regular clientele on Italy's backroads.

The weekend arrives and the men are ogres, drunk and unruly, abusive and mean, and the women complain. But the police don't come – after all, what happens in this part of Italy is an open secret; it's an open-air sex market where newly trafficked sex slaves are trained on the busiest sex street in Europe. The hotels along the road all rent by the hour, and all cater to sex workers, whether they are there by choice or not. I once stayed at a hotel along the road and when I checked in, the receptionist looked at me suspiciously, as if perhaps I was the one committing a crime. She asked for multiple IDs, kept going back to talk to her manager, and finally gave me the keys to a room in a wing where no one else was staying. I walked around the hotel at night and saw a string of Nigerian women and what I assume were paying clients come and go.

Reflecting on the scene, I think about the Nigerian girls I saw on the boat. Is this where they are now? They would technically be adults at this point. Who knows what they have been through by this time, and whether they could be rescued. So many of the women trafficked for sex on the streets of Europe today were brought over as teenagers and very young women, based on statistics collected by UNHCR. And even if they only came over as adults, women who are rescued from the sex trade share a common story of desperation and hope that allowed them to be trafficked. They wanted to believe there were opportunities for them across the sea, and they were willing to do anything – even believe someone they might have suspected was lying to them – to escape. Even if they had heard the stories from anti-trafficking groups and victims, they probably believed it wouldn't happen to them.

Follow the money

Traffickers are not the only ones making money from child sex exploitation. What is rarely discussed is the complicity of the hotels that rent rooms for sex parties in areas where sex trafficking is rampant. This is not unique to Italy, of course. All over the world, sex tourism is aided and abetted by a tourism industry that ignores it. In places like Thailand, which has one of the highest rates of child sex trafficking in the world, hotels frequently offer rentals without questioning clients or alerting authorities. In the mid-2000s, US-based airlines started training flight attendants to recognise people on their planes who were potentially being trafficked. The signs included young women travelling alone with one older chaperone who answered for them and, in many cases, stood outside the bathroom to make sure they didn't reach out for help. Today, across the US there are signs in airports aimed at victims. One, seen in Atlanta in the summer of 2024, says simply: 'He's not my uncle, but he told me to call him that.' It goes on to give warning signals other passengers should watch for and states, 'Human trafficking victims are transported on commercial airlines daily.' Similar signs can be seen in airports elsewhere, including many European countries, but more consistent international efforts are needed to educate those in the travel sector to watch for signs of sex trafficking.

There is a clear line between legitimate sex work and forced sexual slavery. There is also a difference between an adult consenting to take part in sex work and a minor who is being controlled and who cannot, by definition, give their consent. But for the clients, the real entities who enable the criminal side of sex, there seems no clear differentiation. Efforts to educate men and, increasingly, women who buy sex, about their 'product' are also missing from the roster of potential solutions.

While the focus is often on female victims, very little attention is paid to the growing number of male child sex trafficking victims. Yet, despite the growing number of boys literally on the market, many programmes are outdated and focus only on girls when it comes to both awareness and protection, according to UNODC.

'While male trafficking victims are receiving more attention than in years past, social and health services as well as legal and advocacy frameworks still predominantly focus on female victims of sexual exploitation,' according to UNODC's 2022 report. Both mainstream media and civil society groups tend to ignore them as victims, leaving them unseen and unhelped.

In sex trafficking situations, males are almost always the perpetrators; the buyers of trafficked women, the makers and consumers of paedo-pornography. Awareness that males can also be trafficked for sex may be slower to develop. 'Gender norms and masculine stereotypes hinder identification of male trafficking victims,' according to UNODC. 'This false perception plays out in several ways that are damaging to boys and men who have experienced trafficking.'

* * *

In 2022, Italian police, working in conjunction with Chinese police on assignment in Italy, cracked down on a Chinese criminal gang, arresting 33 people for laundering more than $52m in drug trafficking money for the Calabrian 'Ndrangheta organised crime syndicate, tying two of the most powerful criminal organisations in the world together. Ten million dollars in cash was seized from Chinese money mules, as they were called, who ran shadowy brokerages to move money to China.

The drug money arrests led to an investigation that later uncovered a massive prostitution and pornography ring in which underage Chinese girls were being trafficked into and across Europe to work in illegal brothels. Europol reported that more than two hundred victims were identified, and 28 people arrested in Belgium, Switzerland and Spain. Police monitored 3,000 online websites, both on the mainstream internet and on the dark web, that advertised the women, all of whom were marketed as '18-year-olds' available in Belgium, Spain, the Netherlands, Poland and Switzerland.

Each of the known victims, and police admit there were likely more, owed their traffickers between $40,000 and $50,000, which means the traffickers would stand to earn $8m by the time they paid off their debt bondage. The traffickers advertised the girls for hook-ups online, and not on the dark net, and then arranged meetings at legitimate hotels, Airbnbs and short-term rentals. As reported in TheJournal.ie, the price of the room, a commission and the girls' room and board were all deducted from the per-hour charge for sex with the girl, or in some case multiple girls.

It was not only the traffickers who made money; so did the hotels and the Airbnb owners. If they took a different approach, they could actively try to stop trafficking. Just searching through the Airbnb 'help' page dedicated to people who rent out apartments reveals countless red flags. In one post from 2019, a landlord raises the alarm. Becky41 writes: 'I have put some things together since my guests left this morning, and I suspect that the teen girl with the three sketchy men may be being trafficked. I feel terrible. What can I do?' The user also points out that one of the reserving guests had only uploaded a photo of a tattoo to their account, and queried why Airbnb did not adopt stricter identification standards for users. A slew of responses demonstrates that many Airbnb owners have had similar experiences. Airbnb did not comment on the thread, and when I reached out, they sent me their policy, which suggested that any host who suspects trafficking should call their country's national trafficking hotline and can refuse a rental based on suspicion. Ultimately, today many Airbnb apartment hosts never meet the guests, who just use key boxes and other anonymous means to check in. The potential for abuse of the system is striking.

CHAPTER 7

YOUR KIDNEY FOR
A PASSPORT

Organ trafficking

The private patient unit of the Royal Free Hospital in London is decorated in muted tones and adorned with soothing artwork. The waiting rooms on the public side of the hospital are noisy and occasionally chaotic, but things are more tranquil on the private side. The Private Patients Unit has an array of suites used both by British patients who can afford to jump NHS queues and a number of foreign nationals.

Three wings of the massive hospital are dedicated to private care, and a string of the UK's finest doctors conduct their private practices at the hospital in parallel with their regular work under the NHS. The hospital is famous for transplants, conducting some 140 private kidney transplants and 100 private liver transplants each year, despite an attempt in 2009 to ban private transplants across the United Kingdom to avoid the exploitation and payment of organ donors.

This is where Sonia Ekweremadu, the 25-year-old daughter of 60-year-old Ike Ekweremadu, then the deputy president of the Nigerian senate, was treated as a patient on kidney dialysis waiting for a donor in 2022. Private organ donation in the UK is supposed to be limited to immediate blood-tied family members, but Sonia told me in an interview that she carried an AP01 gene, which complicates the transplant process and prohibited her immediate family from donating to her. She told me that her immediate family also suffered kidney problems, which apparently rendered them ineligible.

To help find a donor, her father approached 51-year-old physician Obinna Obeta, who sourced David Nwamini, a 21-year-old street vendor from Lagos, Nigeria. Because Nwamini was donating his kidney to the politician's daughter, the Ekweremadus were able to arrange a fast-tracked UK visa for him. Sonia's father assured the hospital that the young man was compatible after allegedly undergoing rigorous testing in Nigeria, and on arrival it was ascertained that he indeed had the right blood type for the transplant.

At the hospital, he was introduced to the attending doctor as Ekweremadu's first cousin. An interpreter, who was paid around £1,500 for her help by Ekweremadu, acted as more of a broker than an interpreter for the Lagos street vendor, essentially facilitating his coerced consent to give up his kidney, a court would later hear.

When the young man introduced by Sonia's father as her 'cousin' underwent a physical examination, he was determined ineligible for the transplant because the staff perceived him as not understanding that he was going to have an organ removed. Instead of being disappointed not to be able to help his cousin, he was noticeably relieved. Yet the hospital staff did not report the suspicious scene to police.

Only when Sonia's would-be donor went directly to the police did authorities intervene. After being rejected by the hospital, he was taken in by Obeta, who, he said, he feared. He told police that Obeta had lined up the transplant of his kidney for Sonia back in Nigeria, and he was told that he would have to return to Nigeria immediately. Fearful that someone else would try to take his organs, he ran away, sleeping on the street until he had the courage to go to the authorities.

He told police that he 'owed' Obeta his kidney in exchange for a visa and permit to stay in the UK. He now lives under police protection in the UK, and at the time of writing, Sonia is still on the waiting list for a legitimate donor.

The Metropolitan Police's modern slavery chief investigator Esther Richardson said that the donor was 'treated as a commodity', and called the exchange 'a transactional process just like any drugs or firearm deal. Had this been successful, the victim would have had long-term medical implications that may even have had the requirement for dialysis.'

'He is innocent and naive,' Richardson said. 'Having never been on a flight, he was petrified the plane would fall from the sky. When he fled Obeta's flat, he slept on the streets fearing that snakes might bite him at the flat.' It was later determined that Obeta engaged in witchcraft to try to brainwash his victim not to escape, which is a common tool in the trafficker's arsenal, especially in Nigeria where the juju curse is regularly performed on women being groomed for sex trafficking.

After a lengthy investigation, the elder Ekweremadu was arrested, convicted, and sentenced to more than nine years in prison for trafficking the street vendor for his kidney. Ironically, in his home country of Nigeria, Ekweremadu had championed legislation to prohibit trafficking in persons for the increasingly lucrative organ trade. His 56-year-old wife, Beatrice Ekweremadu, was sentenced to four years and six months in prison. Additionally, Obeta was convicted for helping traffic the street vendor. During the trial at Old Bailey, the court heard how Obeta had earlier received a successful kidney transplant himself at the Royal Free Hospital. His donor was also a young man he had falsely presented as his cousin. No prosecutions were ever carried forward on that case, and it does not appear to be under investigation.

The case against the Ekweremadus was the first of its kind to be successfully tried under the UK's 2015 Modern Slavery Act, introduced to crack down on organ trafficking and other forms of exploitation.

'He [Obeta] did not tell me he brought me here for this reason. He did not tell me anything about this. I would have not agreed. My body is not for sale,' Nwamini said. Sonia was not charged with any crimes, and she said she honestly believed the person who was lined up to be her donor was a relative she had never met before.

* * *

The first successful organ transplant of modern times took place in 1950 in Illinois when a kidney was transplanted into a 49-year-old woman from a patient who had died of cirrhosis of the liver. Prior to that, the closest anyone had come was a Swiss doctor who performed the first skin graft in the 19th century.

The World Health Organization (WHO) prohibited the sale of organs in 1987, yet by 2017, according to a Global Financial Integrity report, the global organ trafficking trade was believed to be worth as much as $1.7bn annually. Almost 10 per cent of all organ transplants are from trafficked organs, according to the

Global Financial Integrity think tank, which includes what the WHO estimates to be 10,000 kidneys traded on the black market a year, averaging more than one black market kidney transplanted every single hour of every single day of any given year. In 2008, 78 countries signed the Declaration of Istanbul on organ transplantation and transplant tourism. Though non-binding, the agreement sought to rein in what was quickly becoming the Wild West of supply and demand in the fast-moving world of medical technology.

In a 2021 report to the US Congress, researchers found that the black market price of illicit trafficked organs in developing nations is often between 500 per cent and 1,900 per cent less than in developed nations, where complicit private medical facilities tend to not ask where organs come from, or check whether or not the donor is really a relative and really acting freely.

There are three broad categories of organ donors. Legitimate organ donors may have explicitly agreed to become a donor during their lifetime, for example by joining the NHS's Organ Donor Register. However, many countries, including England, are increasingly adopting an 'opt-out' system, whereby anyone who hasn't expressed a desire to *not* donate their organs can be considered a potential donor at the time of their death.

The second category of donors is those who are trafficked or murdered for their organs. In these cases, the donor does not consent to the harvesting of his or her organs. They may be placed under duress, which can include debt bondage or extortion, and forced to sell a kidney or even a cornea, after which they continue living. Or, in the worst cases, they may be killed for vital organs like their lungs, heart or pancreas. These are sold to desperately sick buyers for large sums of money.

The third general category is a living person who knowingly consents to sell an organ like a kidney for financial gain. This can be done illicitly on the black market, or legitimately, for example to help a loved one or family member. In either case, a fee or expenses are usually paid to the donor by the person receiving the organ.

'Organ trafficking may be facilitated by corrupt officials or criminal groups and may include brokers or other middlemen who connect individuals providing the organ with prospective recipients, negotiate the price, and identify medical facilities where the transplant can occur,' the researchers for the Congressional report found. 'Organ recipients, along with the medical professionals involved in their procedure and aftercare, may or may not be aware of the circumstances surrounding an organ transplant.'

Vicenzo Musacchio, a forensic criminologist with the Rutgers Institute on Anti-Corruption Studies (RIACS) in the US, told me that mafias are often tied to the illicit trade in human organs.

> Transnational organised crime exploits the poverty and precariousness of donors, and develops thanks to the inability of countries to satisfy patients' transplant needs. Trafficking in human beings and organs is certainly a source of profit for the mafias and this is also demonstrated by numerous police investigations and judicial sentences at a global level.

He points to what he calls a complex criminal organisation with middlemen and brokers who supply the organ to potential recipients. But in order to do that, he says, there must be corruptible doctors and hospital officials. 'It is necessary to negotiate the price and have the availability of medical facilities where the transplant can be performed,' he says, which usually means a private hospital or clinic.

He says that trade dynamics depends on whether the 'donor' will survive. In some cases, organs are bought, sold and transplanted in the donor's country, which means the victim forced to donate the organ is not moved across borders. But the person may also be moved across borders, often to a third country 'chosen for its tolerant legislation and the presence of compliant doctors'. Only one aspect is consistent across all three categories, he says. 'The poorest countries provide the donors, and the richest countries are the recipients. The mafias manage the criminal market and act as a bridge between the parties involved.'

That the medical facilities carrying out the transplant may not be aware of the provenance of the organ is the primary problem. In the case of the hospital in London, the protocol to spot trafficked organs worked: a comprehensive interview with the donor was conducted and the transplant was not carried out. But in other hospitals around the world, medical officials turn a blind eye to suspicious circumstances or fail to establish whether the donor has given consent to donate.

Organ trade and trafficking researcher Frederike Ambagtsheer, an assistant professor at the Erasmus University Medical Centre in Rotterdam, has conducted some of the most thorough research in organ trafficking to date. She notes that the seedy world of organ trade isn't as hidden as people think, despite its links to criminal organisations. 'Organ trafficking networks are highly organised with close collaborations between the legal 'upperworld' (medical doctors, notaries, lawyers) and the criminal 'underworld' (recruiters, brokers),' she wrote in a recent report for *The Conversation*.

While it's likely that there are also unreported, hidden cases that do not take place inside medical institutions, the available knowledge indicates that the medical sector is helping to organise and facilitate the trade in human organs. The organ trade is a complex crime and is fuelled by the high demand for organ transplants and rising global inequalities.

Movement across borders is integral to the global organ trade. The patients who travel to international private clinics in search of organs are known as 'transplant tourists', and donors may have travelled too, but in trafficking cases this will have happened far more secretively, often involving people smugglers. Several studies have been conducted on the practice of trafficking in human beings for the purpose of organ removal, known as TBHOR, to shine light on the prevalence of organ harvesting among migrants on the move. Not surprisingly, the most common victim of this horrific trade is the desperate migrant.

In 2020, the BBC interviewed an organ broker who worked out of a coffee shop in Beirut, who sold about 30 kidneys a year from people living in refugee camps in the city's slums who were either desperate to try to get out and cross the Mediterranean to Europe or who just wanted to feed their families. He said he once bought an eye and sold it to a desperate buyer. The deal was facilitated over WhatsApp, including a photo of the eye to see if the buyer liked the colour.

The factors driving the trade are varied, but the fact that ten per cent of the world's population suffers from chronic kidney disease, according to Organ Trafficking Research, drives the market, which has set records in the number of transplants every year for the last decade, as stated by the United Network for Organ Sharing (UNOS) in 2023. Kidneys are the easiest to harvest and sell because people can live with just one. But they are also the most marketable. There are hundreds of thousands of people on kidney transplant waiting lists worldwide, and kidneys are available for only around one-third of them. Mortality rates on waiting lists are high, hovering between 15 and 30 per cent, depending on location. These are factors that allow for the exploitation of desperate people.

* * *

Organs aren't harvested in migrant camps or aboard improvised life rafts. They are harvested in private clinics like that in the Royal Free Hospital in London and similar settings all over the world. Intensive medical expertise is required not only to harvest organs, but to keep them in a fit state for transplantation. Human organs have a short shelf life outside the body. Kidneys, if kept properly, can remain viable for up to 36 hours after removal, and the donor can go on to live a normal life. But vital organs require different care. The donor must be kept alive, usually on artificial life support after being declared brain dead in most legitimate transplants, while the organs are removed simultaneously. The donor is then taken off life support.

Israel, before the war, had one of the highest rates of transplant tourism anywhere in the world, and its hospitals carried out the transplants legally, thanks to a 2008 law that better defined brain death, and worked to make organ donation a civil responsibility. The law, which incentivises cadaver organ donation on death, rewards individuals with prioritised access to organs if they 'participate in procurement efforts'. In other words, the more active people are in getting people to be organ donors, which is logged, the higher up the priority list they are when and if they or a family member need an organ.

Things become murky when organs like the heart are involved. The mere suggestion that people are murdered for their organs implies an unthinkable complicity by medical doctors and hospitals. But a transplant doctor I spoke to in Italy, who preferred to remain anonymous, insists that it is not the transplant doctor's duty to vet the organs they are presented with. In cases of car accidents, for example, the transplant doctor will be told a vital organ is available after a team of specialists verify the organs are healthy while keeping the donor alive on life support. The donor is then taken off life support, usually in accordance with family wishes or living wills, or, in some cases in the UK and elsewhere, government intervention.

In less legitimate cases, vital organs are removed from donors who are trafficked for them, usually sold to desperately sick buyers for large sums of money. Iran remains the only country in the world where buying and selling organs is legal for its citizens, though it is by far not the only country to engage in the procedure. All other countries have banned the practice, at least on paper, but some countries, including China, have been accused by the group Doctors Against Forced Organ Harvesting of executing prisoners to harvest organs for their large population.

Globally, the demand for organs is high and getting higher because of the increase in diseases like cancer, chronic kidney disease and cardiovascular diseases, especially in developed nations. The average wait for a kidney is anywhere from two to three years in the UK, and three to five years in the US. Some of that is because kidney dialysis can keep people alive, so the waiting time reflects the survival rate of the patient rather than the availability of the organs.

Patients wait, on average, less than a year for lung transplants but often die halfway through the waiting period, according to WHO statistics. Lung transplants occur at the rate of over 5,000 a year, according to the International Society for Heart and Lung Transplantation; and figures from Statista show that 2022 was a bumper year for organ transplants worldwide, with 157,494 transplants of all kinds carried out. If you factor in the WHO estimate that ten per cent of those are done with trafficked organs, that means 15,749 organs came from people who either sold them illegally or were killed for them.

Organs are also trafficked on the battlefield, where prisoners of war are killed so their organs can be harvested for dictators and even injured soldiers. Battlefield organ trafficking was a common activity in the Syrian civil war, and has been documented in Yemen, and most recently, the early days of the Russian invasion of Ukraine, where the illegal trade in human organs was well established before Russia's invasion. Back in 2003, the European Union's Social, Health and Family Affairs Committee sent rapporteur Ruth-Gaby Vermot-Mangold to study the issue. She found that 'donor' recruitment practices existed in Ukraine, Russia, Bulgaria, Romania and Georgia. 'Trafficking in organs appears to be extremely well organised and extremely mobile, involving a network of "brokers", qualified medical doctors and specialised nursing staff. Strong links are also established with the police and customs staff for purposes of passport delivery and "secure" border crossings,' she wrote in her final report.

War brings out the worst in humanity, which translates into opportunities for those who thrive and prosper on exploiting other people's pain. An Afghan woman named Delaram Rahmati was living a miserable life long before the US and its allies left Afghanistan and made things worse. She had eight children, of whom two were severely disabled, when *The Guardian*'s Rights and Freedom group caught up with them in 2022. By then she had sold two of her daughters to traffickers looking for young brides and was peddling her own kidney in order to pay the hospital bills and special care her sons required. One of her sons was paralysed and the other was mentally ill. And there was also her bedridden husband, whose medicine she had to finance. 'I was forced to sell two of my daughters, an eight- and six-year-old,' she told the *Guardian* researchers. Each one was worth about $885, but the buyers didn't want them until they reached puberty, which meant she still had to feed them. When *The Guardian* found her a year later, she had sold a kidney for about $1,000 less than what she had hoped, and her oldest daughter had reached puberty so had been handed over to the buyer, leaving her one less mouth to feed. Her husband was still sick, and her sons still handicapped, and the surgery to remove her kidney had left her partially disabled.

The report found that in Afghanistan, after the Taliban regained control, the organ trade was booming. Desperate people could be found waiting outside hospitals, not asking for spare change, but begging for someone to buy their kidneys so they could take care of themselves and their families.

Ahmed's story

Today, Ahmed only has one kidney and is lucky to have both corneas. The Egyptian works at a car wash in Rome and lives legally in Italy after testifying against the doctors who trafficked his organs. His scar has faded to a dull cream colour, but it looks like the surgery was performed with a machete and stitched up by a witch doctor, which, Ahmed told me, is what it felt like.

He was living in Alexandria, Egypt during the Arab Spring uprisings, studying medicine and trying to save money by working odd jobs at the port. His dream was to open a small clinic in a remote village in Egypt where he could help people, raise a family, and get out of the city where violence and unrest had become a daily risk he wanted to escape. But there was little money in the stagnant economy, and corruption meant that the chance to study was not awarded based on merit as much as through connections. Ahmed came from a poor family, so had little chance of getting into a good medical school, even though, he says, his grades merited a place. Instead, he studied at a state university that was part of a larger state research hospital system. He made extra money selling his blood and could still barely buy food after purchasing all the books he needed.

All that changed when one of his professors approached him about moving to Europe, where, he was promised, he could continue his studies and even land a job in a hospital where he would be paid enough to rent his own apartment. Ahmed was thrilled at the mere suggestion and quickly moved into a guest house at his professor's villa, in part to save money and in part because the professor told him this would make it easier for him to sponsor Ahmed's application for a study visa in Europe.

One morning, Ahmed woke up in a small operating room he had never seen before with a 30-centimetre incision on his right side. Blood, which he assumed was his, covered the floor, and he had a splitting headache and excruciating pain on his right side. An IV needle was still in his arm, but the tube wasn't attached to any bag of fluid. When the nurse, who seemingly didn't speak

Arabic, French, or any language he spoke, returned to attach a bag of liquid to his IV, he was sure it was something to kill him. The minute she left, he removed the needle from his arm and made his escape, dripping blood from his fresh wound.

He managed to leave the building from a side door and realised it was a private clinic in Cairo not far from where he was staying with his professor. The outside had no writing, but there were a few symbols, almost like it had been marked out in code.

He didn't dare risk returning to the professor's house, so he went directly to the police and reported the incident. They immediately admitted him into a hospital to recover and posted an armed guard at his door. As he suspected, his kidney had been removed. Several police investigators came in to interview him and look at his incision, which the attending doctor said was done in a professional manner. Ahmed wondered if perhaps they had been keeping him alive in order to harvest the rest of his organs.

Ahmed testified against the professor and the university. He was also able to give investigators information about the secret clinic where the surgery took place, which was later closed down. It had been operating under the guise of a cosmetic surgery clinic, but investigators found operating theatres and sophisticated equipment that suggested organ harvesting was performed there. Ahmed was placed in protective custody, which felt like a prison to him since he couldn't carry on a normal life. He eventually made his way to Libya and crossed the Mediterranean Sea on a smuggler's ship he paid for with money he had saved from the stipend he received under witness protection.

Once in Italy, he was granted asylum based on his protected status in Egypt, but he abandoned his plans to go to medical school and now works with other Egyptians resident in Rome who run a series of car washes.

Ahmed is lucky to be alive. Egypt has become one of the most popular destinations for brokers hunting for organs to sell, according to the WHO. In 2019, bodies of several Egyptian nationals were found tied together floating in the Mediterranean Sea, all of them stripped of kidneys, corneas and in one case their heart. Police opened an investigation into an organ trafficking ring centred in Egypt and discovered that would-be migrants who are the most common victims of coerced organ sale or outright theft are Sudanese and Eritrean, nationalities who could otherwise be granted asylum if only there were viable ways for them to apply in their home countries.

A way forward

The global trade in organs is one of the least understood and most lucrative in the illicit business of human trafficking, with vulnerable 'donors' at the mercy of brokers working on behalf of ultra-rich recipients. Unlike every other form of human trafficking, organs are almost always harvested and transplanted in medical facilities, from private clinics to state-run hospitals the world over.

At the root of the problem is demand. At present there are hundreds of thousands of people worldwide on waiting lists for life-saving organs. Donated organs, on the other hand, are scarce. Half of those on waiting lists will die before an organ becomes available, and many people are buried or cremated with organs that could have saved countless lives.

While no major world religion prohibits donating organs, there are also religious and cultural concerns in many countries that complicate the donation and receipt of organs, including religions that require the burial of a deceased person within a few hours of their death. In the US, Asian Americans (primarily Chinese, Indian and Filipino) make up 8 per cent of organ donor waiting lists, but only a small proportion of the Asian population are on organ donor registries, according to national statistics on organ donors, as set out in a 2023 research paper in the *Journal of Racial and Ethnic Health Disparities*. Among the factors cited for the lack of donors was the importance of those surveyed to include often older family members, who might hold doubts about the practice, in their decision to register.

Legalising the buying and selling of organs is not the answer. However, researcher Frederike Ambaagtsheer suggests that incentivising the donation of organs – from both living and dead donors – could mean that more organs will be available legitimately, which would then drive down the need for the illegal side of the trade. 'A contested example of a possible solution to reduce organ scarcity and avoid black market abuses is to allow payments or other types of rewards for deceased and living organ donation to increase organ donation rates,' she suggests, adding that 'strictly controlled experiments would be needed' to test the efficacy and morality of those schemes.

A case in point might be when a person who has not registered as an organ donor is involved in an accident that leaves their brain in a vegetative state while not affecting the viability of their other organs, including their heart, lungs and corneas. She argues that if the family members are given an opportunity to receive some sort of compensation for the organs, it could save the lives of numerous people. In cases where family members are left devastated financially by the loss of a loved one, Ambaagtsheer believes that an 'incentive' for them to consider donating organs could provide the family with economic security and cut down on the illegal trade whereby people sell or are forced to sell the organs instead.

The stories of Ahmed and Nwamini are shocking, but organ trafficking experts point out that the idea that the trade only happens in organised crime syndicates involving 'physical force – even torture and the execution of prisoners' – is a myth. Researchers with the Organ Trafficking Research group point out that 'organ trade involves a variety of practices which can be placed along a spectrum ranging from excessive exploitation to voluntary, mutually agreed benefits.' They call for data-driven research to distinguish between organ trafficking, transplant tourism and tourism for transplantation, which are three distinct areas, the last being widely acceptable in both practice and ethical considerations by the medical community.

The organ trade refers to people taking payments for their organs, which is a crime punishable by law in almost every country in the world. It is different in the eyes of the law from human trafficking for the purpose of organ removal, which is defined as exploitation by the United Nations Convention Against Transnational Organized Crime. The organ trade can be considered human trafficking only if a person is coerced, deceived or exploited.

Difficulty distinguishing between organ trading and trafficking, and understanding the limits of the law, make it hard to monitor the full scope of the problem. Despite concrete efforts to make sure anyone donating an organ to save the life of another person is not coerced into doing so, even the language of groups hoping to help is often confusing. The updated version of the WHO's Guiding Principles on Human Cell, Tissue and Organ Transplantation says specifically that 'live donations should occur with the donor's informed and voluntary consent and that donors should be provided professional medical care' (Guiding Principle 3); that 'cells, tissues, and organs should be donated, not sold, and that sales should be prohibited, though compensation for donations is permitted'. The difference between 'sales' and 'compensation' here is hard to gauge in part because any compensation to a donor of an organ puts into question whether the donation was for monetary gain or a gesture of altruism.

Follow the money

The black market and crime data-gathering group Havocscope, which is relied upon by governments and UN agencies across the world, keeps a tally on the black market in organ prices based on open-source information, including police reports, government studies and the dark web. In late 2023, they listed the average global price paid to a kidney seller as $5,000, enough to support a family for several years in some developing nations.

The buyer, however, pays on average $150,000. Prices vary according to the country. Brokers in places where organ trafficking is more prevalent, like the Philippines, make no more than $1,500 a kidney, while in places where the trade is less transparent, like Yemen, the broker can make up to $60,000, the group finds. Someone in China will pay around $47,500 for a kidney, while a transplant tourist in Israel will pay around $125,000 (a kidney seller in Israel can net $10,000 per kidney, on average), Havocscope's statistics state.

Vital organs, which require a deceased donor, are naturally more expensive. A lung goes for about $312,650 in Europe, the group found, but what's less clear are the circumstances in which the vital organ donors 'donate' for cash. For those in the organ trafficking business, the real money being made is in the US and countries that do not have the protective layer of a national public healthcare system. In the US, kidneys can go for around $250,000 on the black market, skin around $10 an inch, and a heart, which can only be harvested from the dead, can fetch $1m, according to the *Medical Futurist*.

A recent article in *ACAMS Today* (published by the Association of Certified Anti-Money Laundering Specialists), which exposes money laundering often tied to trafficking, reports that the global average price buyers, or patients, pay is much more moderate. In countries where national healthcare systems exist, private patients with the right connections can expect to pay $30,000 for a cornea, $150,000 for set of lungs, and $130,000 for a heart. Livers go for $98,000 on average.

CHAPTER 8

TROUBLED WATERS

The English Channel crossings

At the height of the COVID-19 pandemic in December 2020, British mother Kimberley Harding (aged 39) and her daughter Leonie (21), from Leeds, were driving a six-bed camper into the UK via the Channel Tunnel when they were stopped on the French side of the crossing. The pair raised suspicion at a ferry stop in Rotterdam by giving imprecise answers to questions about their travel during a widespread lockdown. Only vital supplies and certified medical personnel were allowed to travel freely.

The women said they had been working as travelling nurses in Europe and were planning to return home to the UK in their camper van, which they used to quarantine in accordance with pandemic rules. The story didn't ring true for a number of reasons, although initially none of them were tied to people smuggling.

For one, the women's phone numbers were traced to burner phones, which raised an automatic red flag, especially since carriers in Europe and the UK don't charge roaming fees, making the need for disposable phones obsolete except for people who don't want to be traced.

It was found, on searching the women's names on the British National Health Service roster, that neither was certified as a nurse or even a nurses' aide, despite their documents (which turned out to be false) purporting to be medical licences. Authorities thought perhaps the duo were faking their medical credentials and working illegally, or that perhaps they were carrying vaccines or other medicines in short supply in the UK.

Their suspicions aroused, the authorities were inspecting the camper at the final control to board the car train to cross the Channel when they heard strange noises coming from a storage area under the double bed that spanned the width of the camper. When they lifted it and pulled back a curtain, they found five Albanian adults who did not have visas to travel or stay in Europe or the UK. None of the Albanians had previous work history in the UK and were deported back to Albania without incident.

The women insisted that they had no idea the quintet were in their van. It soon emerged that they did, and that they were not acting alone. They had become caught up in the scheme of a 35-year-old man from Leeds named Christopher Hennigan, who had recruited the women to smuggle the Albanians after they approached him for a loan.

Hennigan gave the mother and daughter the loan and then 'employed' them as smugglers to pay it back, since they seemed an unlikely pair of criminals. Few border guards would suspect the mother and daughter, he assumed, especially during the pandemic, when healthcare workers were in high demand. Hennigan was eventually sentenced to 14 years in prison for unlawfully bringing migrants into the UK, and for exploiting the British women. The mother and daughter were identified as victims themselves, and given suspended sentences and community service.

It was unclear how many people Hennigan successfully brought into the UK before he was caught, but his ties to organised crime groups led authorities to believe he likely sold multiple victims into forced labour and sex rings. According to his criminal record, he had also faced weapons and assault charges.

Schemes that use the same technique as Hennigan's – the sourcing of unlikely smugglers – persist. In late 2023, six people from near Liverpool were arrested for a trafficking ring that dated back to 2018. Andrea Cavanagh, 52, and her son James Liddiard, 30, were named the masterminds of the group that smuggled countless Vietnamese people destined for forced labour in trunks of cars. The scheme used unassuming pairs, including mothers and sons, and couples on day trips to Paris, to ferry the Vietnamese victims across the Channel on the car train. They were helped by the fact that law enforcement fighting mass migration tends to focus on larger-capacity vehicles, including long-haul trucks and camper vans. Those who participated in this particular smuggling ring were paid per person, and the victims were destined to be sold on to labour farms across the UK, according to the investigation dossier filed with Canterbury Crown Court.

The six defendants found guilty of smuggling and trafficking charges all received suspended sentences, after it emerged that they were pressured to move the 11 Vietnamese trafficked migrants to pay off drug debts accrued by the young men in the group. The drug dealers they owed money to wanted the smuggled workers for their enterprise. Disturbingly, rather than treating the 11 Vietnamese people as victims, they were also criminally charged and deported back to France, where they were vulnerable to being trafficked again.

* * *

Traffickers know well that crossing the Channel into the UK is the ultimate goal for many of the migrants who enter Europe via its southern borders in Greece and Spain. During the summer of 2023, when thousands of migrants arrived on the Italian island of Lampedusa, then French Interior Minister Gérald Darmanin called for crisis talks with the UK, since many of those arriving will eventually try to cross the channel. 'A large proportion of the people who cross the Italian border here want to go to Great Britain, which is also an incentive to negotiate with our British friends and in particular develop a European treaty between the European Union and Great Britain,' he said.

Joey the broker said almost everyone he deals with wants to make it to the UK, despite increasing pushbacks. In late 2023, British prime minister Rishi Sunak doubled down on his promise to stop irregular migration and prevent trafficked people entering the UK. An initial deterrent plan to send those who entered without a visa to Rwanda was ruled unlawful by the Supreme Court in London, but even so, the British parliament voted 313–269 in favour of keeping the plan alive in December 2023. The plan saw the UK invest some $300m to send 'certain' migrants to Rwanda on a one-way ticket. No account was made in the plans to ensure that people who were trafficked would be given protection. The plan, which involved sending migrants from all over the world to Africa regardless of their origin, prompted concern among human rights groups. By the time the UK Supreme Court ruled that it wasn't a safe destination for migrants, Rwanda had already received millions of pounds to set up centres to house deportees. The controversial plan was ditched when Sunak's party lost the 2024 general election.

In 2023, dozens of people died trying to cross the English Channel, despite the promise by smugglers on the French side that they would be safe. According to the IOM, the fee to cross ranges from $1,936 to $2,150, and sometimes comes with tips on how to navigate the British asylum interview once they reach the other side. The boats that cross the frigid waters are small and often go undetected among the massive cargo ships in the world's busiest shipping lane.

The number of small boat migrant arrivals has increased significantly since 2018, though it still fluctuates year on year. According to the Home Office, 29,437 people made the crossing in 2023, compared with a high of 45,774 in 2022, but in the first half of 2024, 12,646 small boat arrivals were detected, up 16 per cent from the first half of 2023. While the crossings have become the subject of intense political scrutiny in Britain, the same overall number (for example 29,000, as in 2023) might occur in just a month off the coast of Italy.

* * *

For those who make it to the last frontier of northern France, the UK appears both amazingly close and just out of reach. Migrants who get to the dismal migrant camps of Calais, formerly known as the Jungle, are at the last – and perhaps most difficult – stop in a journey that has been mined with deadly risks. Many have traversed the deserts of Africa, survived torture in the detention camps of Libya or Tunisia, avoided drowning in the perilous waters of the Mediterranean Sea, and navigated the sometimes hostile borders of continental Europe.

Once in Calais, irregular migrants have two means to cross the Channel to England: above water or under it. Those who choose the underground route are mostly known as truck jumpers. Every day, groups of them gather at petrol stations and the last roundabouts before the entrance to the Channel Tunnel and try to jump on to trucks as they slow down to move around the circle. Others stow away when the trucks are parked to refuel or while the drivers are in rest areas. Lorries also cross the Channel on ferries, and stowing away on these is another method some migrants and smugglers use. It's risky, but not quite as dangerous as trying to cross the frigid water by boat.

Some truck jumpers fall to their death; others hide in unventilated refrigerated trucks, only to die of asphyxiation. Sometimes truck drivers know that the jumpers are on their vehicles and try to shake them off by braking hard or turning fast. Open Democracy reports that nearly four hundred people are known to have been seriously injured or killed, their bodies often found by the roadside, between 1999 and 2024. An appeal launched by advocacy groups in 2021 called the practice of speeding up to make the migrants fall inhumane and asked truckers not to react so violently and to not jerk the trucks around to try to throw people off.

Even if jumpers are successful, many will be caught by security guards at the terminals, either because they become disoriented, believe they have already crossed the channel and get off too soon, or because truck drivers realise that there are stowaways aboard and alert officials. Some make it across the tunnel only to be caught on the UK side by sophisticated scanning systems that can detect heat signatures and shadows.

Truck drivers have been attacked. In 2021, a Portuguese van driver was beaten to death when he tried to forcibly remove three Calais truck jumpers from his vehicle. In 2017, a Polish truck driver died when his vehicle crashed into an obstacle that migrants had put in the road to slow the trucks down so that they could jump on.

* * *

As migrants try to find a way across the Channel, traffickers scout for business. Some have money to pay smugglers themselves, but there are plenty of people waiting to give those who don't a loan that will end in debt bondage. 'Pay on the other side, I'll find you a job,' the traffickers assure them. Once they agree, they may never escape the chains of modern slavery.

On a reporting trip to Calais in 2021, I caught up with two young men from Ghana whom I had first met outside the central train station in Rome. I'd used their mobile phone numbers, supplied by Italian aid groups, to keep in touch during the pandemic. When I met Adu and Ali in Rome, they said they wouldn't stop until they reached Brighton. They were inspired by their hero, the British-born soccer player of Ghanaian heritage Tariq Lamptey, who played for both the Ghana national team and Brighton and Hove Albion.

The two were in their 20s and had met on the migration trail. Adu had been a farm worker in Ghana, and Ali a mechanic. Both had lost their father and felt they needed to send money to their mother to help support their family.

Ali was desperately afraid of water, and was convinced he was a good enough athlete to jump on a truck. Adu had suffered an injury in a farm accident and felt more confident about taking the boat. Both men had worked odd jobs and sold counterfeit Gucci bags, worked in farm camps, and begged for money outside coffee bars to earn enough to pay smugglers outright. Neither had been involved with traffickers.

I left the area before either man attempted the crossing. In autumn of 2021 I got a message from Adu. He was in Brighton and had just started working as a dishwasher in a restaurant. He didn't have asylum documents, but there was a community of people who were helping him to apply. When I asked him about Ali, he was silent.

I later discovered from a coroner's report that Ali's lifeless body had been found inside a truck. He had apparently pried open the door of a refrigeration unit on a truck at a petrol station before the terminal. Others who were trying to cross with him heard him banging from inside the truck, but the driver approached and chased them away. One of the men tried to tell the driver what happened, but the driver just got in his truck and started driving. The driver notified authorities at the first checkpoint of the terminal that some migrants were milling around his truck and that he was concerned they might be hiding, according to a police report about the death filed by the Calais coroner. Ali had written down Adu's contact information in case something happened to him, so someone from an NGO in Calais called him to relay the details. His body was buried in a migrant grave rather than being repatriated back to Ghana.

* * *

The Channel Tunnel has presented security challenges to border authorities since its inception. In 2001, several migrants dug under an unpatrolled gated area to breach the terminal in an attempt to walk to the UK along the underwater rail line where trains pass at speeds of around 100 miles per hour. They would put their backs against the walls when the trains passed, but risked being sucked under the moving locomotives. A train driver spotted them as he passed, and alerted the authorities, who then stopped all traffic until they could be found. In all, 44 Afghans were arrested and deported back to Calais.

Between January and July 2015, more than 37,000 migrants tried to cross the Channel through the tunnel system according to the Eurotunnel group, reported in the *Brussels Times*. Often, the attempts involved several thousand migrants at one time trying to push through security blocks. On several occasions, Eurostar trains were prevented from crossing. Eventually, the fences round the entrance to the tunnel were reinforced, making it impossible to breach them without a heavy armoured vehicle.

What's known about the attempts by people to make it across the Channel is primarily because of failures, not successes. The people who do make it across – whether in boats, smuggled among cargo shipments or in car boots – and are undetected are the fodder of great political debate. The British government says that for a variety of reasons it is impossible to know the exact size of the country's irregular migrant population. 'Some people will successfully evade border controls and remain in the UK unde-tected,' the government website says. 'Some people may enter the UK on regular routes and their status subsequently becomes "irregular" – for example, if they overstay a visa.'

Crossing by water presents obvious risks. In early December 2023, seven rubber dinghies carrying a total of 190 people, presumably sent from France by people smugglers, were stopped in the frigid water off France after it was determined that the small boats were being hitched on to large cargo ships, making them harder to detect, but putting them at unimaginable risk. It is unclear how many made it across without being detected. The tiny rubber boats can easily get sucked into a propellor or capsize in the ship's massive wake. The 190 people were part of a group of people a trafficker paid smugglers to get across. Had they been successful, they would have reached the English coast at night, making them harder to spot. Had they been sucked into a propellor, it is probable that no one would have ever found their remains.

According to the UK *Defence Journal* and *The Times*, British and French authorities have started using drones to patrol the waters and identify boats carrying migrants, which has enabled them to rapidly identify small boats and send patrol boats out. But since 2018, more than 100,000 people have made it across alive, as Global Initiative against Transnational Organized Crime reports, potentially lining smugglers' pockets with more than $2m. Smugglers charge between £2,000 and £5,000 for the crossing, depending on time of year, supply and demand, and patrols in the area.

For smugglers, the economic bottom line varies little whether or not the migrants make it across alive. Only those whose crossings are funded using the hawala system will incur losses, as their payments are usually released after they make a crossing successfully. This system is more common for English Channel crossings than for Mediterranean crossings into Italy or Spain. For the traffickers, though, any migrant death en route represents a loss of future income.

For so many, the dream is to get to the UK, but there are rarely solid plans in place if they actually make it, beyond the hope of claiming asylum. They cannot expect assistance from UK migrants who have already been granted asylum because the right to remain and work comes with a catch – if they are caught abetting illegal immigration, they will lose their own immigration status.

Migrants who have made it all the way to Calais without being trafficked have avoided many traps set for them along the way. When they arrive in the UK, however, traffickers are quick to offer assistance, including ready 'jobs' and solutions, including falsified documents, to solve what are otherwise insurmountable problems.

* * *

There are two main groups of people who try to make it into the UK without papers. The first group is migrants or asylum seekers originally from Sudan, Somalia or Eritrea, for example, who might have travelled or been smuggled by the Central Mediterranean route and make their way to Calais to try to cross the Channel. The other is those who have come overland via Turkey or the Balkans, for example if they're from Afghanistan, Syria, Iraq or Iran.

In the year to June 2024, UK government figures show, the largest group of arrivals (17 per cent) was Vietnamese, thanks to a strong broker–trafficker alliance in Vietnam that continues to help shuttle people to the UK in cargo ships and long-haul trucks. (By contrast, two-thirds of the people who have been detected over a longer period since 2018 were from five countries (Iraq, Afghanistan, Iran, Albania and Syria).)

A key route for Vietnamese irregular migrants now is to be trafficked to Serbia first, from where they can more easily be smuggled into the UK. Many can come legally to Serbia on temporary work visas, like the nearly 500 trafficked Vietnamese workers who were found working at the Linglong tyre factory near Belgrade in 2020. The factory said it had hired the workers through a Vietnamese contractor, but what was happening was clearly labour trafficking. Once the young men arrived in Belgrade, their 'manager' took their passports and forced them to work long hours at the factory, according to an *Observer* investigation.

The nearly 500 workers had applied for what they thought were legitimate jobs, but once they arrived in Serbia, they were told they owed the person who got them the work £30,000 each. The trafficking organisations earned some $1.9m for providing the tyre factory with slave labour. The wages the young men earned went directly to pay for rent in their bleak accommodation, which housed around fifty people in each room in dormitory-like barracks.

These young men were trafficked after applying to ads on legitimate platforms, including Facebook and mainstream media, for work abroad. They travelled legally to Serbia on the worker visas provided by the Serbian government based on the tyre factory's letters of employment, but no one ever checked on their welfare after arrival. In some cases, the visas were automatically renewed by the company, and immigration authorities asked no questions.

Minh's story

In a separate trafficking incident, a 16-year-old boy told a *Guardian* reporter how he was smuggled into Dover in a cargo truck in June 2013. Minh (not his real name) knew he was going to the UK, and he knew he would be working, but little more than that. Once in the UK, he remembers being put in the back of a car and driven for many hours before he was locked in a dark house with all the windows boarded up, with rows and rows of grow lights for cannabis plants. He had never seen the plants before and had no cultivation experience, but he did what he was told.

He said he was often visited by Vietnamese men who left him frozen food he had to ration out, not knowing how long it would be until they returned. They also checked on the plants he was tending, criticising him if they weren't healthy. He had no idea if it was night or day since all the windows were blacked out, and said the smell of the cannabis buds made him constantly nauseous. 'It was like another kind of world,' he said. 'I didn't really even feel human. I understood very quickly that the plants were more valuable than my life.'

Police eventually raided the house, which he later learned was in Chesterfield. But rather than being rescued from his nightmare, he was arrested for illegally growing the drugs. Mimi Vu, a social worker who later took on his case, believes Minh was sold by his family to traffickers who then paid smugglers to move him by land via Russia. Vu said that from what he told her, it was clear that he was sold between several gangs on the way and transferred to and from various trucks. He was also sexually assaulted and often beaten.

When he arrived in Chesterfield, he was told he owed the people who brought him to England thousands of pounds, but because he did not speak English at the time, he had no choice but to do what the older Vietnamese men told him to pay back his debt. 'These are just the prime conditions for exploitation,' Vu said. 'The only people these kids know and can rely on by this point are their traffickers, who are in complete control of their lives.'

In the mid-2010s, police started looking for tell-tale signs of the covert cannabis operations, which had put Chesterfield on the map as the UK's largest producer of both legal medical marijuana and illegal pot and hashish. In 2014 alone, police seized 276,676 cannabis plants worth around £62m across the UK, the

Guardian report says. Most were being tended by trafficked kids from Vietnam, like Minh. 'Vietnamese kids have always been trafficked into illegal work, but cannabis is a perfect industry for their exploitation,' Vu said. 'It's easy to conceal someone in an empty house, the police see cannabis cultivation as a low priority, and if they do raid the house, the kid is usually too terrified to share anything worthwhile with them. And they've broken the law, so they're likely to be seen as criminals first and victims second.'

That's exactly what happened to Minh, who was arrested, fingerprinted and charged. He was so afraid that he didn't tell the police that it was his traffickers who forced him to grow the cannabis. And the police seemingly didn't suspect he was trafficked, despite the obvious signs, including that he was locked in the house and living in squalor. At just 16, he should have gone into foster care, but there weren't any spaces available, so he was taken to a B&B and given £30 to buy food until he could meet with a court-appointed Vietnamese-speaking lawyer. His traffickers had always told him that if police found the plants he cultivated, he should try to escape or he would be thrown in jail for the rest of his life.

In his short time in the UK, he only knew them. They were the only people he trusted. And he didn't speak any English, so he felt completely isolated and alone. He took the £30 and got on the first bus he could find. It was going to Sheffield, where he knew no one. 'When I got off the bus, I was in a strange city,' he told the court later. 'Then I began to feel guilty about getting into trouble, so I tried to get back to the house, but by then I didn't know the way back.'

After a few days in Sheffield, scavenging food from rubbish bins and sleeping rough, he was taken in by an older Vietnamese man. For two years, he stayed with the man's family and learned some English words, but he did not have any documents that allowed him to stay in the UK and he was stopped during a random check. When his fingerprints brought up the old cannabis charge, he was taken to prison. And because he was by then 18, he had to stay there.

This time, with the help of a translator, he told the officers about how he had arrived in the UK in the back of a cargo truck, how he was locked into the house and made to grow the cannabis, and how his traffickers coached him to try to escape if he was ever arrested. The Home Office registered him with the National Referral Mechanism for victims of human trafficking. But due to a lack of cross-referencing, he was still brought before a judge to face the cannabis charges. He pleaded guilty with the help of a court-appointed lawyer who had no experience of representing victims of trafficking, and he was sentenced to eight months in the Glen Parva institution for juvenile delinquents in Leicestershire, which was later closed down after being deemed 'deplorable' due to both the unhygienic conditions and the fact that it was a breeding ground for gangs.

Halfway through his sentence, he was set to be released for good behaviour, but the early release was revoked on the basis of illegal immigration charges that were discovered as his release papers were being drawn up. He spent another 13 months being moved between immigrant detention centres. When a social worker finally got a hold of his case, he was set free and provided full protection. His case went before the UK Supreme Court, where all previous charges were removed from his record.

His case prompted a thorough investigation into how he fell through the cracks of the legal system after he was identified as a trafficking victim. Research by the charity Focus on Labour

Exploitation has found that hundreds of victims of trafficking were also in immigration detention centres, which defies both logic and the Home Office rules on victims of trafficking, which say that they should have been eligible for protection. But victims of trafficking frequently do not have a chance to apply for asylum as other immigrants who enter a country illegally might.

Some Vietnamese teenage boys who had been trafficked in similar circumstances to Minh were forced to work in restaurants as dishwashers during their time tending the cannabis crops, meaning they had more contact with the outside world, but no one questioned any aspect of their work or immigration status. Vietnamese girls are often forced to work in nail bars and as prostitutes. Teenagers of both genders are often forced into domestic servitude, where they can be kept out of sight for years.

In the period 2016–2019, nearly five hundred Vietnamese minors, mostly teenage boys, were identified as having been trafficked into the UK, many specifically for cannabis cultivation. Why these children were earmarked for that industry is a subject of debate since cannabis in any form is illegal in Vietnam, but at least half of them were forced to cultivate the drug, which is illegal for recreational use in the UK. Many of them were made to raise the plants in abandoned apartments and deserted warehouses, often living in squalid conditions.

* * *

In December 2023, the last of 40 people were sentenced to prison terms totalling more than 117 years in the UK and Europe for an elaborate trafficking scheme that brought people from Asia via the Balkan route into Europe. The group of men were caught in 2019 after a shipping container from Belgium showed up in a British port with 39 dead Vietnamese people hidden inside a refrigerated unit, as reported by Sky News. The driver who left the corpses at the cargo port had turned off the ventilation and air conditioning early on in the journey, and the temperature in the unit rose to nearly 40°C.

The investigation into the 39 dead Vietnamese people revealed messages between the driver and his boss. Eamonn Harrison, who picked up the cargo container in the UK and noticed a smell, messaged his boss, Ronan Hughes, asking him what to do. 'Give them air quickly, but don't let them out,' he told the driver, who responded with a thumbs-up emoji.

But surveillance footage showed the driver opening the back of the container and taking a step back from the stench and a visible vapour rising from the back of the truck. He called his boss once more, and then 20 minutes later called the emergency services and pretended he had no idea the cargo he was picking up was human.

The main men involved were convicted of 39 counts of manslaughter. Lesser charges were handed down to taxi drivers, port attendants and lookouts who had been trained to evade the authorities while moving the Vietnamese people from safe houses to their so-called 'VIP' cargo container.

Of those victims who had phones on them, the final messages were horrifying in the detail of their agony, including several people writing to family members to tell them goodbye as they suffocated from stifling heat. 'Mom, I think I'll die suffocated,' one woman wrote. Her mother told local media she thought her daughter was headed to the UK on a VIP train to work in a nail bar. Others had been told they were destined to work as hairdressers and gardeners, but they would all have very likely ended up modern slaves.

* * *

Labour trafficking in the agriculture sector has emerged as an area of great concern since the UK's departure from the EU created a shortage of seasonal workers. Before that, it was easier for people to work legitimately in the UK if they were only a resident, rather than a citizen. The peril of trafficked labourers burst into the British consciousness in 2004, when more than twenty undocumented trafficked Chinese workers drowned while harvesting cockles in Morecambe Bay in north-western England. Unfamiliar with unforgiving local tides, the workers were caught off guard while out harvesting the cockles during low tide. Fifteen workers survived, but two bodies were never found.

The investigation into their deaths prompted promises to investigate forced labour in seafood harvesting. The Chinese gangmaster who 'owned' the workers, his girlfriend and a cousin were eventually found guilty of manslaughter and facilitating illegal immigration. They are all now out of prison. But two English men, David Anthony Eden, Sr and David Anthony Eden, Jr, who allegedly arranged in advance to purchase the cockles, never faced legal action.

Forced agricultural labour is a problem across Europe. The southern Italian province of Puglia is where one-third of the country's tomato exports are grown and processed. In the summer of 2021, Italian anti-Mafia police carried out a sting operation in the region of Foggia, where several mafia-style groups reign, that led to the arrest of a dozen people, including a Senegalese gangmaster and several farmers who had hired him to provide harvesting crews for tomatoes and olives. More than 150 workers, primarily African migrants, were identified as the Senegalese gangmaster's 'property'. He was paid by five different agricultural enterprises that had annual revenues totalling around $2.1m, according to the police. By hiring the undocumented, indentured workers, the businesses could avoid paying taxes and insuring the workers. The 150 workers were part of a much wider phenomenon. They were living among thousands of workers in encampments known locally as ghettos. The conditions in encampments are unsanitary, but some are so established many of them have makeshift churches, mosques and even small stores.

Injuries are common among workers employed in these conditions. During the summer of 2024, an Indian national died after his arm was severed during fruit harvest outside Rome. The gangmaster who ignored his pleas for an ambulance and instead dragged him to the side of the road where he bled to death was arrested. The man was part of a country-wide scourge that could have been stopped three years earlier with the discovery of the 150 farm workers in Puglia. Instead, the practice was pushed further underground, making it harder to find. A month after the 31-year-old died, 33 Indian nationals were freed from 'slave-like' conditions by Italian police in the northern city of Verona. Each had paid a broker around €17,000 for what they thought was a valid work permit to travel to Italy for seasonal harvest work, according to the police. But once they arrived, the men were told the work permits were not valid and were charged an additional €13,000 for permits that would legalise their status. They were told if they didn't comply, they could be deported. They worked for around €4 an hour and were contracted out as a team to various farms in the area, police said. The two Indian gangmasters who were arrested when they were freed were found with more than $545,000 in cash, presumably from the work the men did.

Italy's CGIL labour union estimates that throughout the year more than 12,000 trafficked migrants live in seasonal encampments across Italy to carry out tomato, fruit and citrus harvests and production. Because these workers are not documented, they do not qualify for any protection by the government, meaning there are no guarantees for their pay, how many hours they work, or their safety. Black market labour in Italy is a well-documented issue. The US State Department estimated in 2023 that Italy had an estimated 1.5 million unregistered workers and 3.7 million undocumented workers in the shadow economy who are at risk of labour trafficking. At least half a dozen migrant workers have died in Italy in the last five years alone, a police source told me. Most perished in fires that began in the improvised kitchens of the ramshackle slums they were forced to live in. In many cases, the encampments where these undocumented seasonal workers live have no running water, which means no washing machines or indoor bathrooms. 'Migrants worked through gruelling shifts without food, and only have access to well water, even during the hottest hours of the day,' investigating officer Ivano Bigica said of the deaths of migrant workers in the last five years. He told me that the workers were paid between $4 and $8 for each 300kg case of tomatoes they filled rather than by the hour, which is against labour rules in the country. During the height of the harvest season, workers were in the fields between eight and ten hours a day, he said. Workers' pay was docked if they were found to have put any dirty tomatoes in the crates, or if they loaded them incorrectly onto the trucks. They also had to pay for their transport to the fields and for their food. By law, the minimum daily rate for documented seasonal farm workers in Italy is $60 a day, on which they are required to pay taxes, which means a trafficked migrant worker would have had to harvest 3,600 kilos of tomatoes to make the minimum seasonal wage under Italian law.

A way forward

Since 2021, the United Kingdom has seen reports of incidents of human trafficking increase by 10 per cent a year, according to the National Crime Agency. But as the US State Department pointed out in its 2023 report on Trafficking in Persons, in that year the UK prosecuted fewer cases than in previous years. In addition, UK nationals are now Britain's most commonly identified victims of modern slavery and human trafficking; in 2023 they represented 51% of victims.

There are clear guidelines on identifying potential victims, and there has been a concerted effort by the British government to make sure crimes involving migrant workers are thoroughly investigated as potential trafficking cases, but as in so many cases, there is a lack of implementation. Priority is given to stopping irregular migration over saving trafficking victims. The young Vietnamese boy named Minh was identified as a trafficking victim in accordance with legal best practice, but due to a number of inconsistencies in record keeping and priority being given to rooting out illegal cannabis farms and kicking out undocumented workers, that identification was never passed on to the criminal justice system, which treated him as a criminal, not a victim.

There have been positive steps to educate first responders and security forces to take into consideration factors like age, language proficiency and cultural awareness, and when in doubt to activate the investigative protocols that are in place to safeguard victims.

But experts say that wider society also needs to be more vigilant. The demand for various services – massages and manicures, or sex – is what keeps trafficking alive. Nail bars are notorious for exploiting migrant workers, but millions of people still purchase cheaper manicures over expensive spas. Seemingly vacant housing where noises are heard or where people are seen going in and out with groceries should be reported as well.

Often, when trafficked people are discovered carrying out illegal activities, whether growing cannabis or carrying drugs across international borders, they are treated as criminals, not victims. That's what the traffickers want. Many are also penalised for breaking immigration laws, even though so often they are taken across borders against their will.

Governments around the world find it convenient to group irregular migration and trafficking together, and by no means are all people who cross borders against the law trafficked. Many are willingly breaking immigration laws to illegally enter a country. It is often impossible to tell the difference between the two groups, but they require very different strategies in terms of assistance. People who are forced from their homes because of war or extreme poverty deserve a right to request asylum. People who are forced from their homes to turn a profit for a trafficker deserve protection.

Follow the money

The investigation into the five hundred smuggled Vietnamese boys mentioned earlier ended up dismantling a trafficking ring that had successfully brought more than a thousand people into the UK – each having paid, or their traffickers having paid, up to £30,000 each for what was described as exclusive or VIP service from Asia to England. That means the smugglers involved pocketed more than £15m just from those who were definitively tied to the ring. But at least four other attempts at smuggling people from Asia into Britain have now also been pinned to the group, including an articulated lorry that was stopped in France in which there were around twenty migrants from Asia, who escaped along with the driver, that would have netted the ring £600,000. Separately, also in 2019, a gas station surveillance camera caught around 45 people thought to be Asian running from another lorry trailer into a forest. If each paid the same as the Vietnamese victims, the group possibly would have made over £150m in less than three years before being stopped.

CHAPTER 9

AMERICAN NIGHTMARE

Exploitation in the US elite and underworld

A group of nannies from the Philippines stands outside a posh
private school in San Francisco, waiting to pick up their charges.
They don't talk to the teachers, and they avoid making eye contact
with the parents. The other au pairs and parents who are waiting
nearby eye them frostily.

One of the young women, later given the pseudonym Lily in
court documents, has a secret. As she will eventually tell police,
the children she looks after treat her terribly, but the parents
are worse. They beat her and force her to sleep on the floor of a
tiny closet. She is often left alone with the three children for full
weekends.

One of the other nannies she met outside the school eventually
saved her by telling her own employers the story. They reported
the family, and Lily was removed from the home. The parents
were arrested, but as of late 2024, the case is still pending in court
after they tried to cast blame on the agency in the Philippines.

Lily was brought to the US in 2019 through an agency based in
the Philippines that offers nannies tailored to the needs of different
families. The contracts are generally limited to three months and
the agency promises that the nannies are carefully vetted. But

once in the US, the agency has nothing to do with them. In many cases, the women discover that the dream job, which has often come with the promise of full-time work permits, opportunities for education, and free time to discover America, is a lie.

Lily's story is not unique among foreign nannies working in wealthy communities around the world. Agencies in the Philippines often find the nannies in in situations of extreme poverty. They are given little training before they are shipped abroad.

Domestic work is one of the most common of all the forced labour trafficking categories, according to the ILO. In the US alone, it is estimated that 65 per cent of all domestic workers are foreign born, and their immigration status can make them particularly vulnerable to traffickers, according to the Human Trafficking Hotline.

A woman from the Philippines referred to as Nicel in court documents thought she had escaped an abusive family she was working for in London when she took a job with Jose Aguila and Lorraine Lim, a married couple with children, including a disabled son, in San Francisco. The couple essentially ordered a bespoke nanny from an agency that had nannies who could take care of disabled children. But when Nicel arrived, she was made to sleep in a tiny unheated cupboard among storage boxes, and she had to attend to the disabled son 24 hours a day, as well as cleaning the home, taking the other children to school and preparing the family meals.

For the first three months of her contract, she was paid the agreed-upon $240 monthly fee, but then when her contract expired, they started paying her $40 a month. She didn't get any time off, and the couple confiscated her passport, meaning she couldn't leave.

Finally, a neighbour called the police after witnessing physical abuse against Nicel on the property. Police rescued her, removed the children from the home and took the parents into custody. It is rare that abusers and exploiters are arrested. Oftentimes, the trafficked person is removed or deported. But San Francisco District Attorney Brooke Jenkins decided to make an example of the case, asking people who had domestic help to take a closer look at the workers' friends to determine if people were either being held against their will or exploited in other ways. 'Domestic workers play an important role in our economy and like all workers should be paid fairly and protected from exploitation,' Jenkins said in a statement, as reported by CBS News. 'Domestic workers are particularly vulnerable to exploitation and trafficking due to their isolation within their employers' homes,' Jenkins said in court. 'Our office stands with the victim and will do everything in our power to hold Jose Aguila and Lorraine Lim accountable and send a message that this conduct will not be tolerated.'

The couple face up to 19 years in prison if convicted.

Sherile and Edith's story

The enclave of West Harrison, Westchester County, New York, is a quintessential dormitory town, housing New York City's elite. Foreign nationals in the upper tax brackets especially like the private village, about twenty miles from Manhattan, known for its massive colonial-style mansions and gorgeous manicured front gardens. The little town is bordered by a lake and a moderately tall hill, meaning it will never grow beyond its current quaint size, and will remain exclusive. The population, just below 30,000, is primarily wealthy and predominantly white. Home values average

$2.5m, but a lakefront property can cost as much as $10m. Tax records show that most families employ domestic help.

On an average weekend morning, the small hamlet's three country clubs are abuzz with couples taking tennis lessons, businesspeople golfing, and kids doing supervised activities. Up and down the residential streets, gardeners clip hedges and mow lawns. Inside massive homes, full-time maids polish marble floors and make sure everything is in order for weekend dinner parties.

Two of these domestic workers, Sherile Pahagas and Edith Mendoza, worked at different times for the German diplomat Pit Koehler. Koehler was a German envoy to the UN who – perhaps ironically, it transpired – focused on human rights abuses. Pahagas and Mendoza sued Koehler and his wife Marieke in 2017 for allegedly trafficking them to the US, not paying their promised wages, and maltreating them. The accusations against them included not letting them see a doctor when they needed one, and confiscating their passports.

Pahagas and Mendoza brought the landmark cases when they met by chance in a park in New York City after each separately escaping the Koehlers. They found a lawyer, and were able to get the rights group Damayan Migrant Workers behind them to fight for their cause. Even though they ultimately lost the case, due to the Koehlers' diplomatic immunity, the case was widely reported, prompting scores of workers from the Philippines to come forward to share similar stories of horrific abuse, some of them also at the hands of diplomats across the world. It is notable that the judgment to drop the case specifically states that 'nothing in the defendants' motion to dismiss based on diplomatic immunity challenges the factual allegations of the complaint.' In essence, the case had credibility in the eyes of the law, but could not be tried under the rule of law.

Originally from the Philippines, Pahagas and Mendoza had both applied from abroad for a job as live-in housekeeper and nanny for the Koehler family in New York. Both were thrilled by the prospect of living in America

Pahagas arrived in New York from Hong Kong, where she had been working as a domestic worker, in November 2012. She thought it was a dream come true when the taxi pulled up to the Koehler estate. But she soon found out that she was expected to work up to 100 hours a week for around $4 an hour. She stayed on the job for two years and finally quit in 2014. Pahagas said at a rally held in support of their case in August 2017 that she had been lured to the US under false pretences. 'They fooled me into thinking I could come to the US to make good earnings for my family at home, but it was all lies. The Koehlers treated me like a slave.'

Mendoza's circumstances were similar; she too was recruited from abroad to take Pahagas' place. She worked for the family for just one year before being fired in 2016 after a doctor told her she needed a week off work to rest. The two filed a federal complaint on 28 June 2017 with the US District Court in the Southern District of New York.

Both women had originally signed a contract to work for 35 hours a week, Pahagas for $9.86 an hour and Mendoza for $10.02 an hour. They were each supposed to get paid time and a half for overtime, but neither ever made more than $350 a week for around 100 hours of work. The women each approached the family during their employment, according to the complaint. In both cases, the family then grew distant, sometimes not speaking to either woman for days.

According to the complaint, they were forced to care for four young children, including waking to soothe them at night; cooking all meals, including at weekends; daily deep cleaning of the six-bedroom, six-bath house, and the garage, and taking care of some maintenance work, including shovelling snow in the winter. They also had to iron clothes, do the grocery shopping, and drive Mr Koehler to the train station after getting the kids on the school bus. Most days started at around 6 a.m. and ended just before midnight. Saturdays were often longer, if the family hosted dinner parties.

The women, who had been granted work visas, were told by the family that if they left employment, their work visas would be revoked and they would be deported. The family also assured them they would make sure no one else would hire them. In the end, even though their case was dismissed, both were granted long-term visas to build their lives in the US under the legislation in place for human trafficking victims. Mendoza went on to speak out on behalf of trafficked labour workers in the diplomatic community.

Reena Arora, the women's lawyer, told the court that the women were ignored, dehumanised and forced to work gruelling hours. 'You're asking someone in your household to be working between 90 and 100 hours per week – and they're completely isolated, they're in a mansion in Westchester, they don't have access to public transportation, they have only one day off a week, when their health is in jeopardy and they're penalised for trying to seek medical attention, they're not given any days off, they're being paid woefully under what the promised rates were,' Arora told the court that would eventually dismiss the case. The two sought damages of $368,402.94 for unpaid wages and legal fees and although they won nothing tangible, their case started a long-overdue conversation about the prevalence of indentured servitude in some of the most elite communities, one of the most common forms of 'upperworld' human trafficking in the US.

* * *

It may seem surprising that the abuse of domestic workers would occur in wealthy and privileged 'upperworld' settings, but sadly this is a common theme. The diplomatic community is a case in point. Worker exploitation has been a problem in that circle for decades, according to a 2016 report by Duke University that blames a system of protectionism and elitism that often prohibits workers from coming forward out of fear.

There are countless agencies catering to diplomats, arranging visas and recruiting young women for jobs as domestic workers, which are frequently investigated for their role in human trafficking, according to the US State Department. 'This is a rampant practice, in my opinion,' Reena Arora told ABC News, saying that the problem persists where there are diplomatic enclaves, both in the US and in diplomatic cities like Brussels and Geneva. 'This is a problem in D.C., which houses most of the embassies, and in New York, which houses the United Nations. We see a lot of these cases come through.'

In October 2022, a Kuwaiti diplomatic attaché to the Permanent Mission to the State of Kuwait at the United Nations and his wife were charged with forced labour and visa fraud after three domestic workers from the Philippines and India filed a complaint with the Southern District of New York. This time the charges stuck, in part because two of the workers claimed to have been physically abused, while the women working for the German diplomats were not. The diplomat, Barrak Abdulmohsen Alhunaif, and his wife, Khaledah Saad Aldhubaibi, both returned to Kuwait and remain at large in the eyes of the court.

The phenomenon is not just an American problem. In June 2024, the Hinduja family, considered one of the wealthiest in the UK, were convicted by a Swiss court for exploiting vulnerable domestic workers, as reported by Die Welle. Prakash Hinduja and his wife Kamal were each sentenced to four years and six months in prison and their son Ajay Hinduja and his wife Namrata were given four-year jail terms. Additionally, the family's business manager was given an 18-month suspended sentence. The court asked why a family that owns the Hinduja Group, which has interests in banking, oil, media, healthcare, entertainment and chemicals, would need to traffic illiterate workers from India, confiscate their passports, and force them to work 16-hour days in their Geneva home for less than 400 francs a month, which is 90 per cent less than what they should have earned in Switzerland. The answer? Because, until one worker escaped and reported them, no one stopped them.

* * *

While trafficking workers into wealthy homes represents an 'upperworld' route to the US, it has many 'underworld' equivalents. In late 2023, Department of Homeland Security authorities noted a worrying pattern. What it called 'pseudo legitimate travel agencies' were advertising organised trips through Facebook, Telegram and other internet sites to potential irregular Asian and African migrants. The travel packages took clients to the Mexican border with the US via Nicaragua and Ecuador, both countries that faced geopolitical strife, including food and energy shortages, and the ousting of Ecuador's president in 2023.

Historically, irregular migrants who try to enter the US by land were often from Central and South America. Now, increasing numbers are coming from China and Senegal. In 2023, nearly 10 per cent of migrants attempting to cross the border into the US were not from Latin America, according to an investigation by Reuters. A decade earlier, that number was less than 1 per cent.

Once the migrants arrived in transit countries like El Salvador, Ecuador and Nicaragua, the 'package travellers' were hooked up with smugglers who took them to the US border checkpoints in groups of up to a thousand people at a time. There, they were joined by traffickers who either recruited new victims who were out of money, or sought out specific people whom their trafficking network partners had sent on the trips.

Most of the Africans trying to get into the US in late 2023 and early 2024 were from the West African country of Senegal, thanks to the fact that several of these agencies had popped up in Dakar. Because the travel packages sold are for legitimate travel, either on charter flights or regular airlines, authorities could do little to stop the scheme, even though it was clear that the final goal for many travellers was to enter the US illegally.

The establishment of the Nicaragua route to the US prompted a spike in irregular migration from Senegal; the number of Africans apprehended at the southern border more than tripled between 2022 and 2023. The UNHCR did not note any decrease in the number of people from Senegal trying to cross into Europe during this period. Senegal is not a 'refugee-producing' country by the UN's definition, meaning that migrants trying to take the South America route will have a difficult time applying for asylum anywhere along their route, and can easily be exploited.

It is unclear to what extent these pseudo-travel agencies act as cover for trafficking recruitment centres, and to what extent their 'customers' are being induced or controlled. US Homeland Security officials say they have no access to law enforcement investigations in the countries where the schemes operate, meaning the connection between traffickers and the agencies is assumed but not proven.

At the time of writing, the travel agencies sold itineraries which involved taking connecting flights leaving Dakar via Casablanca, Madrid and El Salvador before arriving in Nicaragua. Because Nicaragua does not require a visa to enter, just a simple permit that costs $10 and can be bought at the arrival airport, few checks are made along the way. It is virtually impossible for travellers to leave the airport in Madrid; those who have tried have been deported back to Senegal.

In early 2024, a similar scheme emerged; would-be US immigrants were taken from China to Ecuador, so that they could take the land route along with other people trying to enter the US. CNN documented a number of bus services that could be seen advertising passage to the Colombian border with signs written in Chinese.

Once migrants make it through Colombia, they cannot avoid crossing the Darién Gap, which the Council for Foreign Relations describes as one of the most dangerous migration routes in the world. More than sixty miles of it is undeveloped, the only road gap between the Pan-American Highway, extending from Prudhoe Bay, Alaska, to Tierra del Fuego off the southern tip of South America. The section between northern Colombia and southern Panama was never completed, in part because the terrain is just too rough to work and the rainforest is protected.

Indigenous communities and criminal gangs live in the lawless area. There is no mobile phone service, no bridges and no formal infrastructure.

Years of irregular migration have worn footpaths through the vegetation, but they are regularly swallowed up by thick mud from the seasonal torrential rains. When authorities do venture into the area, they frequently find bodies, though these represent only a fraction of those who die in the wilderness. According to the French NGO Médecins Sans Frontières (MSF), 124 bodies were recovered between 2021 and 2024, far short of the number of people reported missing during that time frame. Those who die while making the crossing are often swept away in the rivers or attacked by a myriad of wild jungle animals and river creatures. Some are killed by other migrants or members of the criminal groups that prey on those passing through. MSF set up a field hospital on the Panama side of the Gap in 2023, and reported stories of young children being swept away in rivers, injured people being left on the side of the trail, and a prevalent smell of decomposing bodies on the route.

A 40-year-old man called 'Oscar', who MSF workers interviewed in their Panama camp, described the crossing as a 'nightmare with 1,001 demons'. Columbian by birth, Oscar departed for the US from Bolivia, where he had been living. 'I saw a child get dragged down the river when he let go of his parents' hands. I have seen dead bodies, drowned, four of them. I have smelled corpses decomposing in the ravine,' he told the group, describing how at one point he was lost for 14 days before finding the trail again. He also described the criminals he encountered along the way: 'Some were dressed in black, with shotguns, others wore balaclavas and had rifles and knives. They raped three of the seven women in our group. We were assaulted twice by different gangs.'

Deep in the rainforest, criminals and a vast group of under-world 'helpers' or 'coyotes' are everywhere. They are largely funded by cartels – criminal organisations who work together to dominate drug or other illicit trades. They control supply in order to fix prices. Cartels work in much the same way as organised crime syndicates and mafia organisations in North Africa, the Balkans and Italy to source victims for traffickers. The cartels offer what amounts to a porter service for migrants with enough money. Those who can't pay upfront will be offered the service on credit, and compelled to pay it back either in cash or in kind at a later date. For all the apparent chaos on this leg of the migrant trail, those who are indentured rarely escape, assuming they survive: even if they do, there is a good chance their traffickers will find them, even when authorities can't, as the NEXUS Institute found.

In 2023, more than half a million people crossed the Darién Gap jungle headed for the US, according to a report by UNHCR, over three times more than the number of people who crossed the Mediterranean, according to UNHCR records. (Three times as many people died on the Mediterranean route.) Most paid around $150 for help to cross the Darién Gap, meaning that their 'helpers' made some $75m.

It's not just traffickers who make money from the migrants. Several NGO groups have noted that in the last few years, temporary housing for travelling migrants has even sprung up on either side of the deadly pass. Along the way, local people and officials profit from the Darién Gap crossing in various ways. But like all lucrative markets, the cartels and organised crime syndicates of Central and South America hold the real power, and eventually all the profits filter through to them.

Not unlike the smugglers and safe-house owners who profit from those who cross the desert to arrive in North Africa to cross the Mediterranean Sea into Europe, local governments along the way through Central and South America all profit from the Darién Gap crossing, with many people leaving their jobs to provide assistance to migrants, which has proved far more lucrative. 'What was first a problem has become an opportunity,' a local politician who charges $40 a person to cross dangerous rivers in the jungle told *The Week*, pointing out that in doing so he's not breaking any laws: he does not transport people over any borders, but rather delivers them nearby where someone else can take them the rest of the way.

Once in Mexico, smugglers engage in increasingly dangerous methods to move people into the US, including hiding them under tarps on the top of cargo trains, and stuffing them into small boats to be pushed across the Rio Grande, usually in remote areas, which makes it difficult for US Customs and Border Control officials to intervene.

In the spring of 2023, a CNN television crew travelled the Darién Gap with several groups of migrants, sleeping rough and navigating the murky world of cartels who control the territory. Of all the difficult stories they chronicle in the documentary that grew from the journey, the hardest to forget is that of Haitian Jean-Pierre, who was carrying his sick young son Louvens. They paid the cartels who control the territory to cross without fully understanding the difficulty. 'Strapped to his father's chest, he's weak and coughing,' the correspondent Nick Paten Walsh says. 'But Jean-Pierre pushes on, their fee already paid. There is no going back. Their home of Haiti – where gang violence, a failed government and the worst malnutrition crisis in decades make daily life untenable – is behind them. And impossible choices lie ahead.'

Along the way, cartel members yell advice. 'Take care of your children! A friend or anyone could take your child and sell their organs. Don't give them over to a stranger,' one says as a group trudge through the thick mud. Dead bodies are cast aside, skulls and bones protrude through dried mud. The fastest-growing demographic is Chinese people, authorities say. How they get to the starting point is unclear, but it seems most fly in on tourist visas.

All along the route people are forced to pay the cartels, who essentially sell them on to other cartel members. Some young women disappear entirely, likely taken off the trail and sold into sex slavery. The young women are all told to carry condoms because of the likelihood of being raped by the cartel members. There is no justice in the jungle, and those who make it to the final clearing are physically weakened by the journey. There is literally no way to go back – the route is one way. They have no choice but to move forward and try to make it to the US border.

A way forward

Whether they arrive through 'upperworld' immigration schemes like trafficked domestic workers, or via 'underworld' routes like the Darién Gap, irregular migrants who do make it across the US border are extremely vulnerable and face an uncertain future.

Of all the forms of labour trafficking, domestic servitude is often the most difficult to spot because the work is so often done in private houses, behind closed doors. It also thrives on the fact that the entire sector is over-reliant on informal, cash-in-hand agreements. As a result, it is very poorly regulated in almost every country, with workers not given paid time off or sick leave, which makes it easier for abusive employers to deprive workers of their liberty. Live-in workers are the most vulnerable, since their employers can control their movements.

Domestic labour trafficking is defined by the Organization for Security and Co-operation in Europe (OSCE) as 'subjugation, intimidation and an obligation to provide work for a private individual, excessively low or no salary, few or no days off, psychological and/or physical violence, limited or restricted freedom of movement, denial of a minimum level of privacy and health care.'

Formalising work agreements, a way to provide protection for those who are privately employed in the domestic economy, is often impossible. Without it, workers have little basis on which to ask for help. But more needs to be done at national level to protect domestic workers. In the US and UK, labour laws governing domestic workers are extremely strict. In the UK, foreign domestic workers can get a visa for two years, and are supposed to be given a written contract that includes overtime pay, time off, and other work benefits. But given the extensive evidence of domestic workers who are being exploited, it is clear that not everyone follows the established rules. A recent study by InfoMigrants found that one out of ten domestic workers in the UK have suffered the consequences of modern slavery.

There are 'visitor visas' under which diplomats in particular bring in foreign workers. These visitor visas either explicitly or indirectly exclude domestic workers in certain categories under certain conditions, and some visas allow an employer to 'sponsor' a worker by taking full responsibility for them. That means a would-be domestic worker trafficker can provide a work contract that is in compliance with labour laws when it comes to hours and pay, but because they are the worker's sponsor, they alone control whether the contract is honoured.

In the US domestic workers are often not protected under fair labour acts, under civil rights acts, or even under discrimination regulations for employment. A domestic workers' 'bill of rights' would be a good starting point for tackling exploitation and trafficking among domestic workers, according to the American NGO Polaris, since that would provide enforceable frameworks and give victims more power to negotiate for better wages and working conditions.

Temporary work visa systems also contribute to the ease with which domestic workers are trafficked, according to anti-trafficking groups. Many domestic workers are allowed to enter foreign countries if they are 'sponsored' for work, and most of these visas are non-transferable, meaning workers can't leave an abusive or exploitative situation without facing deportation.

Beyond creating a federal domestic worker bill of rights that has provisions for leaving an abusive situation without facing deportation, Polaris has several recommendations to end this sort of trafficking, such as changing visa regulations for this labour sector that keep people tied to their traffickers out of fear; creating an awareness campaign to highlight red flags; and instituting codes of conduct for diplomats posted in foreign countries that would compel them to follow anti-trafficking laws.

There are many ways a trafficked domestic worker falls through the cracks, starting with the social circles many of these workers are part of. If a non-trafficked childcare provider in a legitimate work situation knows how to spot a trafficked person who may be accompanying children at parties or playgrounds, that person could be flagged, rescued and eventually saved. But if people within the victim's own community are also too afraid to raise the alarm, the practice will continue. Educating all domestic workers to watch out for their peers who may be in trouble is one of the suggestions anti-trafficking groups would like to see implemented.

In 2023, the *New York Times* carried out an investigation of child labour in factories that make some of the US's most beloved brands. They found 15-year-olds packaging Cheerios in a factory in Grand Rapids, Michigan, most of them having been trafficked to fake relatives on family reunification visas that weren't properly vetted. Across town, they found other unaccompanied minors, who had been 'reunited' with relatives they didn't know, working for the Hearthside Food Solutions factory, which processes Chewy and Nature Valley granola bars and packages snacks like Cheetos and cereals like Lucky Charms – foods the kids doing the packaging should have been enjoying instead.

The investigation found underaged trafficked child labourers in every single state, from 12-year-olds working as roofers and construction workers in Florida and Tennessee to minors working in slaughterhouses in Mississippi and North Carolina, to kids sawing wood in lumberyards during the graveyard shifts in South Dakota. 'In town after town, children scrub dishes late at night. They run milking machines in Vermont and deliver meals in New York City. They harvest coffee and build lava rock walls around vacation homes in Hawaii. Girls as young as 13 wash hotel sheets in Virginia,' the report found. 'They bake dinner rolls sold at Walmart and Target, process milk used in Ben & Jerry's ice cream and help debone chicken sold at Whole Foods ... middle-schoolers made Fruit of the Loom socks in Alabama. In Michigan, children make auto parts used by Ford and General Motors.'

All of the kids in the report were registered as unaccompanied minors who had crossed the southern border with Mexico on their own. Most came via the Darién Gap route, according to the Center for Strategic and International Studies (CSIS). The only other way into Mexico is via a paid ferry service or flights, which are inaccessible to irregular migrants. Under the Biden administration's policy to move children out of shelters and into foster care or with relatives, no matter how distant, many of these unfortunate children instead fall into the hands of traffickers, who get the government stipend for their care while forcing them to work 12-hour shifts. Many of the kids are also required to go to school by day under the conditions of their permits to stay, meaning they arrive at school exhausted, overworked and ignored. 'As the government, we've turned a blind eye to their trafficking,' Doug Gilmer, the head of the Birmingham, Alabama, office of Homeland Security Investigations, told the *Times*.

Follow the money

Forced domestic labour is one of the most difficult sectors to quantify. People who are exploited aren't always trafficked, and those who are often remain invisible. It is hard for anti-trafficking groups to explain why a wealthy diplomat would traffic a domestic servant to the US or UK when they can usually afford to pay the generally low salaries.

'It is about power and control,' says Lillian Agbeyegbe, a learning and impact manager at Polaris. 'The domestic worker workforce, both globally and in the United States, is largely comprised of migrants. However, of the victims of employer-traffickers who reported their immigration status, only 19 per cent were undocumented, meaning 81 per cent came to the United States legally under the auspices of non-immigrant visas. This, however, does not prevent them from becoming trafficking victims.'

Those who exploit people without trafficking them most often do it for economic reasons, either to cut corners on employment taxes or to just save money, Agbeyegbe says. Wealthy people who traffic impoverished people or migrants are a different case. In the case of diplomats, they might be following cultural norms, engaging in classism or racism that is also evident in their home countries, or have used corrupt agencies who are making the profits.

Attorneys Rees Broome clarify the legal position for domestic workers as follows: In the US, domestic workers should be paid the federal minimum wage, which in 2024 was $7.25 an hour, and they should be paid time and a half for any hour over 40 a week. But there are many exemptions from the rules. Certain categories of domestic workers, including casual babysitters (who are not trained professionals) or companions for elderly people who are not medical workers, are exempt and can be paid less, according to the US Department of Labor. Live-in domestic workers are also exempt from the overtime payment requirements as long as they live at their employer's home permanently or for an extended period of time, like weekdays. These exemptions create loopholes for those wishing to exploit workers, and undocumented migrants are often the most vulnerable because they need the work, but for a variety of reasons do not qualify for legal alien or green card status.

CHAPTER 10

PIG BUTCHERING

The new cybercrime frontier of trafficking

Anti-trafficking groups were alarmed to find that trafficking
not only continued but accelerated during the global COVID-19
pandemic, as reported by the US State Department and Global
Initiative against Transnational Organized Crime. Restricted
movement dealt a blow to forced labour and sex trafficking but,
ever adaptable, traffickers in many parts of the world innovated,
entrapping those whose financial situation was most impacted by
stalled economies, and turning to forced online criminality and
cyber scams. Once COVID restrictions were lifted, many of these
cyber scams continued, some employing people who had started
out working from home but had then been lured to in-person
sites. The US State Department estimates that this new form of
modern slavery has now grown into a multi-billion-dollar two-
fold industry, one in which the trafficking victims are made to
carry out the crimes.

Cyber scam trafficking is the most significant emerging facet
of human trafficking, according to a 2023 US State Department
report, and one that is increasingly difficult to get a handle on, in
part because it has gone largely unnoticed outside victim support
circles, enabling it to cover its tracks. Unlike more traditional

forms of trafficking, victims of cyber scam trafficking can more easily work indoors, hidden away. Like the Vietnamese children forced to cultivate marijuana in the UK, victims of cyber scam trafficking can be housed where they are forced to work, making it less likely they will be discovered in the way someone forced to harvest vegetables in open fields or sell sex on the street might be.

Cyber scam trafficking victims are forced to carry out cybercrimes, making them vulnerable to prosecution if they are discovered. Cyber scams can take many forms: one model has the perpetrator develop an online romance with a victim in order to trick them into giving up their money, often to cryptocurrency schemes in which unsuspecting victims make sham investments based on false hopes that the person who is scamming them is actually a potential romantic partner. Unlike sex trafficking, there is rarely sexual contact between the perpetrator and the victim, though when a trafficked person is carrying out the scam, they can be vulnerable to sexual abuse.

The COVID-19 pandemic drove what the State Department called in its 2023 report on trafficking in persons a 'pivot toward widespread use of human trafficking to perpetrate these crimes'; and in the wake of the pandemic lockdowns, NGOs working in South East Asia found tens of thousands of trafficking victims forced to work as cyber scammers in 'scamming compounds'. In some cases, more than a thousand people were being forced to carry out scams in these compounds. Between thirty and sixty people might be working in each scamming office, filling buildings of up to ten storeys. Satellite surveillance imagery collected by the Human Research Consultancy (HRC), an NGO doing some of the most in-depth research on the new form of modern slavery for governments and law enforcement, showed large compounds that have active internet and electricity, but no movement between buildings, most of whose windows are completely covered from the inside.

The group, which provided evidence for the 2023 US State Department report about this emergent form of trafficking, calls cyber scam slavery a form of organised crime of 'unprecedented severity and scale'. Consider for a moment the last time you received a suspected scam approach. It could have been online via email, through a suspicious text message, or perhaps someone dialled your personal mobile phone and started up a conversation; maybe they offered you an investment opportunity or a deal on cheaper utility bills. The HRC has found that many people behind these calls are forced to make the calls, hoping for a victim to bite. 'While getting spammed with fraudulent messages is now an everyday occurrence, this inconvenience may actually be rooted in a malignant new form of modern slavery,' the HRC group says in a 2022 report.

Because these scam centres operate virtually, they are very difficult to trace. During the pandemic, certain countries suddenly became hotspots for cyber scam trafficking; Cambodia and Myanmar are two of the primary destinations, according to the research done by HRC. People have been identified and eventually rescued from the Bokor Mountain region in Cambodia and around the Bassac River on the border between Cambodia and Vietnam. Victims have also been identified in Laos, the Philippines, Dubai and Nepal, though rescues remain elusive. Beatriz Silveira, a former Interpol Cybercrime Intelligence Officer, explained to me in an interview that most victims who are flagged reached out to the people they are actually forced to scam for help, making it a complex dynamic in which a cyber scam victim is the key to rescuing a victim of cyber scam trafficking. Needless to say, the trafficking victim is taking a huge risk by raising the alarm and they – or their family – may face severe punishment for doing so.

In Cambodia, many cyber scam compounds are housed in abandoned casinos and hotels. Cambodia banned gambling in 2019, but a number of casinos had been built, often with Chinese investment, in previous years. The gambling ban left these hotel and casino owners desperate and, with very little possibility of selling off their property, many became entangled in organised crime networks with cybercrime arms. Some hotel and casino owners assumed or were told that the groups were opening legitimate call centres and readily signed on, only to find themselves complicit in the criminality going on inside their properties. But some casino owners knowingly made the transition to housing online scams, NGOs have found. 'Hotels and resorts were turned into offices for lucrative scamming activities,' HRC said in its 2022 report. 'Wealth makes corruption possible; corruption allows criminals to operate with impunity.'

Some of the early victims forced to carry out these scams were former hotel and casino employees from China, but by 2023, victims from Taiwan, Hong Kong, Vietnam, Bangladesh, India, Indonesia, Sri Lanka, the US, Georgia, Russia, Malaysia and Thailand had been identified inside Cambodia's scam compounds. Most victims were between 18 and 30, the report found. Victims were restricted in movement, paid meagre wages from which they had to pay for room and board and fees for things like 'keyboard wearing' and 'floor wearing' and, in one case, 'air-breathing'.

Complex dynamic

According to the 2023 State Department Trafficking in Persons report (TIP), South-East Asian NGOs estimate that tens of thousands of people were lured into cybercrime during the pandemic by answering apparently legitimate ads on job websites and social media. The traffickers used fake job descriptions to entice people who could initially 'work from home' during lockdowns, which was enticing especially to people who traditionally worked in other fields.

Once 'hired' by the traffickers, their jobs were to carry out internet scams and tap into banking systems under the guise of telemarketing, carrying out audits and other controls from their own homes, often using software provided by the scammers. As the employment went on, many were then forced to pay for the software, computers or other equipment the scammers gave them. Eventually they were told that they were committing crimes and the only way they would not be arrested was to either continue or move to the headquarters, often in South East Asia, many of the rescued people told investigators and NGOs.

Once there, they were closely guarded, and often beaten and raped if they tried to escape or if they tried to signal to a potential victim that they were being forced to make the calls, according to an international investigation highlighted in the US State Department's 2023 annual report on people trafficking, as outlined by CSIS.

Neo Lu's story

In late 2023, the *New York Times* exposed a scam labour camp in Bangkok where a Chinese office worker had been kept against his will for seven months. Neo Lu (not his real name) was 28 and working in an office in China in June 2023 when he answered an advertisement for a translating job at an e-commerce firm in Thailand. He applied for the visa, quit his job and took what he told the paper he thought would be an opportunity of a lifetime, allowing him to save enough money to eventually move to Europe. Upon landing in Thailand, a driver picked him up at the airport, but rather than driving into Bangkok, he was taken to a labour camp in a jungle encircled by razor wire fences, where he was put in a low-rise barracks with barred windows, guarded by rifle-wielding men in combat fatigues who watched over him as he was forced to carry out accounting tasks. He said he was forced to watch over the criminal organisations day-to-day profits, amounting to millions of dollars in illicit income.

He says he tried in vain to convince his traffickers to let him go, but each time he protested, he was physically and psychologically punished. Eventually, he gave in. 'The scam groups need to give trafficking victims the illusion that they could work their way out of this system,' he told the *New York Times*. 'Eventually the donkey goes from trying to avoid getting whipped to chasing after the carrot dangled in front of them.'

The young man was one of hundreds of thousands of people trafficked for cyber scams. The OHCHR, as outlined in a 2023 report, believes that around 120,000 people in Myanmar and 100,000 in Cambodia alone are living in horrific conditions and being forced to carry out cybercrimes, including running fake gaming websites and cryptocurrency investment schemes, as well as so-called 'pig butchering', which amounts to faking romantic relationships to carry out online fraud, often targeting elderly widows and lonely men. The fake romance schemes took off in China in the late 2010s, and the targets, or 'catfishing' victims, are often American or European. The scammers, whether trafficked or not, create false social media profiles and dating sites that cater to a certain type of victim. The scammer then 'fattens up' the target, softening them up by manipulating them into thinking they are in a relationship, before asking for money, such as for a plane ticket to finally meet in person – which never happens – or to join a cryptocurrency investment scheme. In the first four months of Lu's captivity, he tracked more than $4m in profits stolen from 216 victims, he says. He has no idea how many other accountants like him were tracking other profits.

The scams are lucrative and tend to take place in countries where they are hard to trace. In the case of investment crimes, the victims are often given small sums of money early on to lend their scammers authenticity and collect bank information. Some of the scammers have even built elaborate websites to back up their false identities. The trafficking victims are under constant surveillance so they can't tip off their victims about what's really going on.

The UNHCR blames the pandemic lockdowns and social media for the explosion in this type of trafficking. 'In recent years, Southeast Asia has seen exponential growth in digital technology, business and e-commerce, specifically cryptocurrencies and online gaming as well as increasing digitisation and "app-ification" in the region,' it says. The use of digital payments, which became increasingly normalised during lockdowns, also contributed to the acceleration.

Trapped at home due to pandemic travel restrictions, desperate jobseekers who couldn't work remotely from their usual jobs were targeted by traffickers who were able to convince them to give up personal identification documents, including copies of their passport or ID. Once the traffickers had engaged their victims in cybercrimes, the documents were used to blackmail them; the traffickers threatened to report them for committing crimes in order to prevent them going to the authorities. In some cases, traffickers made the jobs seem lucrative so that when COVID restrictions were lifted, many of the victims were physically recruited to onsite cyber farms. There, they were forced to continue their illegitimate work, only to be later prohibited from returning home because their documents had been taken from them under false pretences, for example that they had to be photocopied as part of the work contract. 'Unlike other traffickers, however, scam operations target educated victims with exploitable skills – like English or Chinese proficiency, or a technological background– and promise attractive salaries for customer service jobs, IT, computer programming, and related industries,' CSIS said in an interview tied to the State Department claims. 'Scam operators usually pay for workers' travel, but upon arrival, confiscate the victims' passports and demand the victim pay back their debt.' Some scams involved online sexual exploitation. And, as in almost every case when victims meet their traffickers, the engagement is 'often accompanied by physical and sexual abuse, restrictions on movement, and starvation.' For example, female victims who couldn't meet their scam quotas by posing nude on online dating encounters were then forced into in-person sex work.

The victims of these victims lost a tremendous amount of money. In the US, the FBI says that American businesses lost more than $2bn to cyber scams in 2022 alone.

The trafficked individuals are manipulated and brainwashed to believe that they will get into trouble if they seek help, and in the case of cybercrimes, the victims are also committing crimes, which the traffickers know will keep them trapped, according to UNODC. What distinguishes those caught up in cyber scam trafficking scams from some other trafficking victims is that by victimising others, they are forced to employ the very tools that keep them trapped.

A way forward

In January 2023, responding to increasing complexity in the global financial fraud landscape, the World Economic Forum launched its cybercrime atlas, an interactive map that tracks cyber scam compounds, victims and law enforcement to create a network, in part to track overlapping enterprises. Once clear networks are defined, law enforcement groups, including Interpol, can work towards arrests, difficult as that often is. Those who traffic people for cybercrimes use the same tools as other types of trafficking for recruitment (preying on emotional or psychological vulnerabilities, promises or threats, theft of documents, kidnapping), but the challenges are very different since the crimes victims are being recruited to commit are virtual, long-distance and contactless. It's difficult for a trafficking victim in this instance to signal they need help. A woman trafficked for sex might ask a client to take her to the authorities and a person trafficked for forced agricultural labour might approach a neighbour or farmer. It is entirely different for someone being forced to commit a scam to ask their victim for help.

A huge problem in combating cybercrime is closing the skills gap between those who carry out these crimes and those who are tasked to stop them. The world's economies are all moving toward greater digitisation, which aids cybercriminals, Interpol says. But the global industry is lacking about 3.4 million cybersecurity experts, according to the World Economic Forum, all people who could help track and potentially stop the crimes if only they had the specialised training.

Europol has focused special attention on the dark web, which allows perpetrators to share information, make deals, and buy and sell people without detection. And because so much content is disseminated far from where the physical servers are, it can be difficult to track down where the crimes are taking place, Interpol says. Cyber child sexual abuse is also a crime that has grown substantially, according to Europol investigations, especially what's known as live distant child abuse, which entails a client paying to watch live-streamed abuse on demand, with the option to make requests about what they want to see.

Staying underground and undetected involves a high level of technical knowledge, and cybercriminals continue to outpace those trying to stop them. In addition, technological developments are leading to new and complex forms of cyber exploitation. A notable increase in AI-generated child sexual abuse material has made it harder to identify what's real and what's artificially generated. While it may seem on the surface that AI-generated child pornography means fewer children are being abused, even fake abuse objectifies and sexualises children, and can inspire real abusers. It also makes it more difficult to identify real victims. 'Technologies such as deepfakes, nudifying, de-aging, artificial intelligence-embedded peer-to-peer file sharing and voice cloning continue to amplify and extend existing methods being used for malicious purposes to exploit children and produce child sexual abuse materials,' Mama Fatima Singhate, special rapporteur on the sale, sexual exploitation and sexual abuse of children, found in a report submitted to the UN General Assembly in 2024. 'More than 96 per cent of pornography generated by artificial intelligence was produced without the consent of the individual featured.' To address these emerging challenges, the gap between offenders and cybersecurity and law enforcement agencies needs to be narrowed, fast.

Follow the money

The World Economic Forum estimates that globally, victims of cyber scams lost $1 trillion in 2023. An Interpol alert the same year warned that in addition to targeting South East Asia, a growing number of cyber scammers were recruiting further afield, targeting individuals from South America, East Africa and Western Europe.

The same year, an Interpol operation carried out in Central and South America, Turquesa V, revealed that victims were trafficked out of the region to Cambodia. A hundred individuals from Brazil were enticed by social media advertisements promising high-paying jobs in the cryptocurrency industry, complete with bonuses, meals and accommodation. However, on arrival, they were trapped and coerced into participating in fraudulent online investment schemes.

The scams the victims were forced to carry out included fraudulent sales in which credit card information was taken but goods were never delivered, illegal gambling and investment scams where the victims were forced to target often wealthy elderly people by taking their banking information and draining their accounts, according to the investigators who carried out the Turquesa V inquiry.

The most common scheme victims were forced to engage in was pretending to be in fake romantic relationships through online dating sites in order to steal money for their traffickers. Nearly 20 per cent of the victims met the person who exploited them on a mainstream dating app or website. Generally, the scammers wanted to quickly exit the dating app and move the conversation to WhatsApp, Google Chat or, increasingly often, Telegram messaging. Scammers often say they have medical bills or travel expenses and they often ask for money through crypto currency or cloud-based banking systems, which are harder to trace.

Artificial intelligence is also emerging as a successful tool for bilking money out of victims. In 2023, an American man was convinced to send more than $60,000 to a lover he met on a dating app, but the love was an AI-generated robot that used a cloned voice, according to the American Association of Retired Persons.

The online apps used most often are Facebook, Instagram, Bumble, Tinder, Hinge, TikTok, Match.com, Dating.com, eHarmony and OkCupid, according to the FTC investigation. It found that 50 per cent of all traffic in which someone reached out to an unknown person was generated by scammers in foreign countries, with Russia and China being the top sources. Once contact was made, the scammers used email and messaging services to appear more genuine.

POSTSCRIPT: A WAY FORWARD

Human trafficking is one of the oldest trades in the world. For much of human history, according to Medievalists.net, slavery, legal throughout much of the world until the 19th century, made the trade in and movement of human beings without their consent a largely accepted enterprise, as outlined by the Exodus Road. Today, human trafficking takes many shapes and happens in both developed and developing nations. Whether sexual exploitation, forced labour or organ trafficking, the scourge continues, and the question of accountability persists, as the OHCHR explains.

That the last major international protocol on human trafficking – the UN's 2000 Protocol to Prevent, Suppress and Punish Trafficking in Persons – dates back 25 years is perhaps telling. A quarter of a century has gone by, during which new facets of human trafficking have evolved. When one considers that the first smartphone came out in 2007, with all the revolutionary changes this brought, it is clear that the existing protocol cannot contend with fast-paced technological advances in the recruitment and movement of victims across borders, as acknowledged by a 2020 Europol report. Most countries do have up-to-date national policies and programmes for helping trafficked people once they are identified, but given the international nature of trafficking, a more integrated approach is vital.

There are countless ways we can all do our part to avoid complicity in human trafficking. First, learn what trafficking is and how to identify potential victims. All 170 countries that are signatories of the UN's protocol on trafficking are required to have dedicated hotlines, informed authorities, and outlets to report trafficking to. You can take this further by fundraising for relevant charities or volunteering to help with anti-trafficking efforts in your community

Become an informed consumer. Learn about supply chains, especially in the fashion industry and fresh agriculture produce. Where does your designer bag come from? Who picked your tomatoes? If you are a healthcare provider, an educator or work in the travel sector, make sure you know how to recognise a potential trafficking situation. Is a young person travelling with someone who does not seem like a relative? Does that person answer for the younger person or restrict their movement? If you are a parent, make sure your children are informed about the dangers of answering unsolicited social media messages or talking to strangers. Are any of their friends vulnerable?

As we've seen throughout this book, the financial sector is one of the weak points in the fight against human trafficking. UN protocol does require banks to monitor and report suspected illegal activity, especially tied to money laundering, which often goes hand in hand with trafficking. Several protocols are in place around the world that allow financial institutions to share information while keeping privacy in place, but traffickers often outsmart the algorithms designed to catch such activity. Banks and financial institutions are also urged to train their staff about what to look for, and the red flags that go with these suspect accounts, the US State Department advises.

Ultimately, efforts to understand trafficking as an industry with complex causes and to humanise its victims is the first step to tackling the problem.

Resources

These organisations can provide information and help to victims:

CIS – Commonwealth of Independent States
e-cis.info

CoE – Council of Europe
www.coe.int/trafficking

EU – European Union
www.ec.europa.eu/anti-trafficking

ILO – International Labour Organization
www.ilo.org/global/topics/forced-labour/lang--en/index.htm

IOM – International Organization for Migration
www.iom.int/counter-trafficking

OAS – Organization of American States
www.oas.org/en/about/who_we_are.asp

OHCHR – Office of the High Commissioner for Human Rights
www.ohchr.org/EN/Issues/Trafficking/Pages/TraffickingIndex.aspx

OSCE – Organization for Security and Co-operation in Europe
www.osce.org/secretariat/trafficking

UNHCR – United Nations High Commissioner for Refugees
www.unhcr.org

UNICEF – United Nations Children's Fund
www.unicef.org/child-protection

UNODC – United Nations Office on Drugs and Crime
www.unodc.org/unodc/en/human-trafficking/index.html?ref=
menuside

**Further information about human trafficking for domestic servitude
is available on the websites of these specialised NGOs:**

AFRUCA – Safeguarding Children (UK)
www.afruca.org

Ban-Ying – Specialised counselling centre (Germany)
www.ban-ying.de

Break the Chain (US)
www.breakthechaincampaigndc.org

CAST – Coalition to Abolish Slavery and Trafficking (US)
www.castla.org

CCEM – Comité Contre l'Esclavage Moderne (France)
www.esclavagemoderne.org

FairWork (Netherlands)
www.fairwork.nu/english

FIZ – Fachstelle Frauenhandel und Frauenmigration (Switzerland)
www.fiz-info.ch
Human Trafficking Pro Bono Legal Center (United States)
healtrafficking.org/resources/the-human-trafficking-pro-bono-legal-center

Kalayaan (UK)
www.kalayaan.org.uk

LEFÖ – victims' support organisation (Austria)
www.lefoe.at

MRCI – Migrant Rights Centre Ireland (Ireland)
www.mrci.ie

Pag-Asa (Belgium)
www.pagasa.be

Other organisations:

Association of Certified Anti-Money Laundering Specialists
(ACAMS)
www.acams.org

Association of Certified Financial Crime Specialists (ACFCS)
www.acfcs.org

Council on Foreign Relations
www.cfr.org

Cyber Scam Monitor
cyberscammonitor.substack.com

Damayan Migrant Workers Association
www.damayanmigrants.org

Doctors without Borders/Médicins sans Frontières
www.msf.org

EuroJust
www.eurojust.europa.eu

Euro-Med Human Rights Monitor
euromedmonitor.org/en

Financial Coalition Against Child Sexual Exploitation
(FCACSE)
www.icmec.org/fcacse

Gabriela USA
www.gabrielausa.org

Humanity United
humanityunited.org

Human Rights Observers
humanrightsobservers.org

Human Rights Watch
www.hrw.org

Human Trafficking Legal Center
htlegalcenter.org
US-based pro bono centre that works to connect victims of human
trafficking to legal experts.

International Centre for Missing and Exploited Children (ICMEC)
www.icmec.org

International Domestic Workers Federation
idwfed.org
Present in 63 countries: advocacy and research in support of
domestic workers' rights and protection.

International Labour Organization (ILO)
www.ilo.org/global/lang--en/index.htm

International Organization for Migration (IOM)
www.iom.int

Interpol
www.interpol.int/en

Meter
associazionemeter.org

Migrant Offshore Aid Station (MOAS)
www.moas.eu

National Center for Missing and Exploited Children (NCMEC)
www.missingkids.org/home

National hotlines for victims of trafficking (Europe)
home-affairs.ec.europa.eu/policies/internal-security/organised-crime-
and-human-trafficking/together-against-trafficking-human-beings/
national-hotlines_en

Pilipino Workers Center
www.pwcsc.org

Rights4Girls
rights4girls.org
A human rights advocacy organisation for girls and young women.

Terrorism, Transnational Crime and Corruption Center (TraCCC)
traccc.gmu.edu

United Nations Office on Drugs and Crime (UNODC)
www.unodc.org

Walk Free
www.walkfree.org

ACKNOWLEDGEMENTS

The toll of human trafficking is often drowned out by our own complacency. It's too difficult and time consuming and complicated to do anything about something that doesn't concern us directly, we might think at first glance. But in the years spent researching this book, interviewing the characters whose agonizing experiences help illustrate what trafficking really is, the one thing I am sure of is that we are all complicit. We all contribute in some way to the scourge, whether through the products we buy, the people we hire, or by doing nothing when there are plenty of ways we could do even the very least.

My hope with this book is that it opens the eyes of those who do want to help in some way, to light a tiny spark, to expose the dark corners of this horrific trade in human lives that happens without exception and often without retribution.

This book would never have come to be if not for the dogged determination and caring guidance of my amazing agent Vicki Satlow, who keeps me focused and motivated. She is a true miracle worker who somehow finds the needle in the haystack every time I come at her with a mess of ideas.

Vicki and Joachim Schnerf of Editions Grasset in France helped me reign in a thousand scattered threads to produce a concise roadmap for the project.

Thank you goes especially to my editor Sarah Braybrooke, publishing director of Ithaka Press, whose thoughtful and thorough editing process helped guide this book to its completion. Her persistence and steady hand enabled me to flesh out vague ideas and find focus on the crux of what I was trying to say.

I also thank all the individual editors of the foreign language editions who helped guide me to the bespoke chapters and alterations that I hope make this book relevant to all who read it, no matter where they might be or in what language.

A book like this relies on many people who cannot be thanked by name, especially investigators and advocates for trafficked people whose work depends on their anonymity.

I thank the victims whose stories I learned so much from whose identities need to be protected and whose courage to move from victim to survivor, and often to advocate, serves as an inspiration to me.

Thank you to my colleagues and editors at CNN whose diligence and journalistic excellence push me to be my best.

And finally, my sons Nicholas and Matthew, who have always given up time with me so I can pursue my journalistic goals, not just now but throughout their whole lives. They have given more for the success of my career than anyone and I am so proud of the young men they have become.